Everyday Architecture: A Vast Wasteland?
Kenneth M. Moffett
AIA Emeritus

ORO Editions
Publishers of Architecture, Art, and Design
Gordon Goff: Publisher

www.oroeditions.com
info@oroeditions.com

Published by ORO Editions

Copyright © 2025 Kenneth Moffett and ORO Editions.

All rights reserved. No part of this book may be reproduced, stored in a retrieval system, or transmitted in any form or by any means, including electronic, mechanical, photocopying of microfilming, recording, or otherwise (except that copying permitted by Sections 107 and 108 of the US Copyright Law and except by reviewers for the public press) without written permission from the publisher.

You must not circulate this book in any other binding or cover and you must impose this same condition on any acquirer.

Author: Kenneth Moffett
Book Design: Bhagwat & Yamuna (@chaitanya_agency)
Project Manager: Jake Anderson

10 9 8 7 6 5 4 3 2 1 First Edition

ISBN: **978-1-961856-87-5**

Prepress and Print work by ORO Editions Inc.
Printed in China

ORO Editions makes a continuous effort to minimize the overall carbon footprint of its publications. As part of this goal, ORO, in association with Global ReLeaf, arranges to plant trees to replace those used in the manufacturing of the paper produced for its books. Global ReLeaf is an international campaign run by American Forests, one of the world's oldest nonprofit conservation organizations. Global ReLeaf is American Forests' education and action program that helps individuals, organizations, agencies, and corporations improve the local and global environment by planting and caring for trees.

for
Lily-Rai

We used to build civilizations. Now we build shopping malls. Bill Bryson

I think that the environment is lousy, and there is hardly any place in North America that the hand of man has touched that it hasn't ruined. Charles Moore

Contents

008 Introduction:
A Vast Wasteland?

010 / 001
All about Sales

1a. Shopping Centers
1b. Drugstores
1c. Assorted Stand-Alone Purveyors
1d. Big Boxes

024 / 002
Dining & Other Amusements

2a. Restaurants, Bars, and Breweries
2b. Fast Food
2c. Shopping Malls
2d. Entertainment

040 / 003
Institutions

3a. Branch Banks
3b. Churches
3c. Civic Buildings and "Civic" Buildings
3d. Hospitals and Clinics

056 / 004
Private Life in the Burbs

4a. McMansions: The Settings
4b. McMansions: The Outsides
4c. McMansions: The Insides
4d. Smaller Houses in the Burbs
4e. Buildings with Many Bedrooms
4f. "Mobile" Homes

088 / 005
Architecture on the Move

5a. Cars and Their Domains
5b. Gas Stations
5c. Industry
5d. Other Architecture on the Move

106 / 006
Open Spaces

6a. Parks and Places Like Them
6b. Campuses and Places Like Them
6c. Sports in the Outdoors
6d. Open Space Gone to Waste
6e. Out in the Countryside

120 Conclusion: Glimmers of Hope

122 Author Statement

introd
vast wa

Architects receive a lot of professional press periodicals (or we used to before they started only sending out digital simulacra of their magazines), which feature building projects that suit the editors' sense of what's considered excellent at the moment. But the trends of the moment are not our mission here, instead we're interested in the 95% or so of buildings that, by and large, never make the cut of being considered notable. This is everyday architecture in the USA, the unsung and ubiquitous masses of buildings that line our streets and parking lots.

    Is it fair to call this a vast wasteland? That memorable phrase was originally coined as an assessment of the television fare in 1961 by Newton Minow, then chair of the Federal Communications Commission. (And despite a choice of thousands of channels and services instead of four – vast indeed – on balance one might well say the same today.) In any case, a lot of what we see or, more to the point, usually fail to see on the way past, is pretty bad. Certainly not all of it; there are workmanlike buildings that do a good job of filling in the background, and there are occasional gems that get to be center stage for a while. While these deserve our admiration, the rest deserve a fair measure of dismay.

    We do tend to look past all the rest; it becomes a blur, failing to garner our attention and often deservedly so. If we're in the suburbs, we're likely to be driving past at a brisk pace so there's hardly an opportunity to observe in any case. And in the last analysis, such observing of the built environment is simply not in the nature of most citizens' way of life anyway; like the frog in the pot with the water getting gradually hotter, we've gotten used to things and simply don't notice how bad the built environment has become.

uction: a wasteland?

So, let's have a look, principally in the darker reaches of ordinary, everyday American suburbia, at several types of everyday architecture. Except for the mega-scale of shopping centers, malls, and hospitals, these tend to be stand-alone buildings. Some of them, to be sure, are pretty big, but most sit in the streetscape or the landscape with space all around them, which is often asphalt paved. Some of these building types will also be found in the centers of cities, where property values will have reduced, if not eliminated those peripheries. Out in suburbia, though, most of them assert a very American quality of independence, each, as Harold Hill the Music Man said of each bassoon, having its big fat say. But, as Don Alhambra in Gilbert and Sullivan's "The Gondoliers" would have it, "when everyone is somebody, then no one's anybody!" Or in more urbanistic terms, buildings in the 'burbs line up with little sense of ensemble or context, each an ill-formed, isolated statement, ending up a sort of vague built chaos. With some trepidation, let's check them out: we may even uncover some everyday work done well, diamonds in the rough out there in the wasteland.

al
abo

While commerce nowadays seems to be mightily focused on the online world, there's still a lot of brick-and-mortar business going on, out there among the big boxes and little boxes and in between. And most of them seem at least a bit unsatisfactory in one way or another, or both.

ut
sales

001

Everyday Architecture: A Vast Wasteland?

1a. Shopping Centers

Shopping centers are an appropriate enough introduction to the subject of everyday architecture generally, since many of the other types that follow have some similar attributes, among them flattish roofs, synthetic stucco walls, and parking lots out front. An internet search for "shopping center architecture" reveals a variety of flashy modernist works, but these are not our subject. As distinguished herein from shopping *malls*, a different animal discussed elsewhere, shopping centers are agglomerations of shops and stores attached one to the next, sometimes bent around in a sort of "U" shape focused on the centerpiece, the sacred parking lot. Often enough these now tend to house a forlorn assortment of placeholder outlets, second-hand stores, and call centers, when they house anything at all. Configurations vary, of course, for they may be Us, or Ls, or just Is, in which in the latter case they will have devolved into the even more ubiquitous "strip centers" (Fig. 1.1).[1]

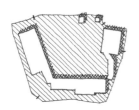
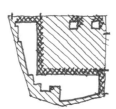
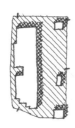

1.1
Shopping center plans: Us, Ls, Is.

In each case one sometimes finds smaller "outparcels" out in front and these branch banks, fast-food outlets, and the like become the public face of the centers beyond. Some more recent incarnations of the shopping center, in addition to featuring the likes of Kohl's, PetSmart, and Old Navy, may include one or more all-too-aptly named "big box" stores like Walmart or Target. For some reason this transforms them into "power centers."

The enduring nature of such places, in addition to their pride of place being given over to parking, is the location of their service entrances at the outer edges of the property (Fig. 1.2). This does mean that the loading docks and dumpsters are out of sight from the retail entrances, but it also means that most of the periphery of the property features nothing but those building backsides. Sometimes, by the luck of the draw, the service precincts of adjacent properties will adjoin, such areas thus imposing their scruffy nature only on each other. But otherwise, as is the case often enough, the back doors of one end up being the view from the front doors of the next.

There is something very American about the frontal parking lot, arising as it does from our love affair with the car. The actual retail entrances are very much a backdrop in these places, but one can hardly gainsay the logic of pulling into the parking lot, parking, and proceeding from there in visible, linear order to the retail

---

1 A reimagining of the strip center concept has been the so-called "office/distribution" development, tenants being anything from printing outfits to nonprofits to mysterious labs. Each slice in the strip comes equipped with a roll-up door in the back, such places being primarily intended for outfits with inventories. But many tenants seem to end up there mainly because the rent is cheaper, despite getting what they pay for.

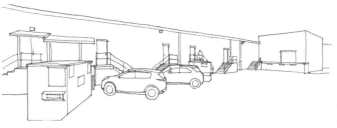

1.2
A shopping center backside.

All About Sales

1.3
Corner shops in Westwood Hills, Kansas City, MO.

destination. In contrast, back in true town centers dating from the turn of the last century, emporiums of commerce looked at each other across Main Street and parking was parallel, or angled, or back behind the buildings. "New Urbanist" schemes from late in the last century onward have promoted updated versions of this pedestrian-forward arrangement, with some success in a scattering of modest commercial centers, all comprising what's really a new look at old urbanism.

But the enduring logic of parking lot fronted shopping remains hard to talk developers out of.

As a youngster, the author ran small grocery errands to a quaint little roadside store embedded in the neighborhood, fronting a corner junction with a bit of angled parking and houses on the other three corners (Fig. 1.3). It was a middle-class version of the corner market still seen in many inner-city neighborhoods. And it was the prototype of what would become, in a much debased and much less walkable form, the strip center, its front parking expanded back from the street by 100 feet or more. Returning to the "new" idea of moving most of that parking to the rear or the middle of such a commercial block, this would have the benefit of shop entrances once again honoring the arriving pedestrian consumer rather than the arriving consumer's car. That said, it's true that such schemes must either have back as well as front entrances, or feature passageways leading to the front, with clever screening of the dumpsters. In the author's own experience in at least two occasions, a developer was actually amenable to parking at the rear of a proposed suburban retail development, only for this well-intentioned ideal to morph, slowly but surely, into relatively tasteful versions of parking-forward centers. They're hard to stamp out.

But encouraging examples, of a sort, do exist. Two, which, admittedly, have clearly benefited from enhanced budgets appropriate for their upper-middle-class patrons, are the commercial townlets of Freshfields Village enroute to Kiawah and Seabrook Islands, and, at a smaller scale, WaterColor

1.4
Watercolor Crossings, Watercolor, FL: not that unusual, perhaps, but a big step up from the usual.

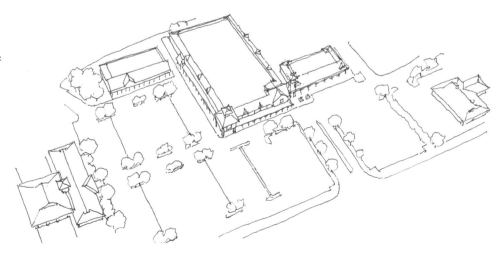

Crossings, adjoining the Florida panhandle beach resorts of WaterColor and Seaside. Neither is all that different in scale from a good-sized shopping center, but they do what they can to subdivide the buildings, the parking lots, and the backsides (Fig. 1.4). In short, the basic design idea is a "village," abetted, to be sure, by a fair dollop of thematic stage setting, but in a good way.

It's nice that we have a few of those charming village-y shopping centers that are carefully designed to meet some actual building design standards and show how such things can be done well, but in general, the standard for shopping center design remains quite low. In typical cases their shortcomings begin at the street, where the destination is heralded in advance thanks to a looming pylon sign-of-signs: no one can read this except for the big one on top, but it doesn't matter because you already know where you're going. Then comes the parking lot and the shops themselves, or rather their front entrances and front entrance signages. It's unlikely there will be any sidewalks, aside from along the entrances, for we must share the pavement with the cars, submitting to their dominance.

There will be a fascia above, often clad in "Dryvit" (see chapters on McMansions for further discussion) extending across the front of the place and emblazoned with the name of each mart of trade. These names comprise a nearly unsolvable problem of graphic presentation. There is no problem involved in making and attaching these names; the problem arises in making them presentable (Fig. 1.5).[2] Should they vary according to each seller's corporate design (or if there is no such thing, the whim of the lessee), the theory being a vibrant variety of color and form? The result is likely to be chaos, to no benefit of the seller, the buyer, or the random passerby. Should they be in the same font and color, all lined up? There will be no joy in such a prison of repetitive dullness. The best one can hope for in typical circumstances is some version of the former that achieves, somehow, a measure of space between the logos, but it will still be chaotic. It could be worse--and often is-- as when there is a mansard or a false half-roof instead of a fascia, with dimensional signage precariously propped up there, appearing to be the afterthought that it sort of is.

Much of the problem of these signs resides in the very continuity of the fascia (or rooflet). One attempt to deal with this has been to further amp up the architectural detail with trims, panels, bands, plaques, and cornices, constituting a quixotic effort to tame the graphics by imposing a riot of Dryvit bits and pieces. Such efforts often come with staggered cornice heights and façade depths as well (Fig.1.6). A more productive and less stage-set approach would be to divide and conquer, rendering the storefronts

---

2 Even some big chains have names and logos made up by laypersons who know next to nothing about corporate identity graphic design. Food City, a supermarket with stores across the south, has an enduring logo, rumored to have been designed by a founder of the brand, that has been vividly described as an "F sucking C." And the name (not the logo this time, but the name itself) of Toys"R"Us (the R is actually backwards on the logo) was the quite odd brainchild of the company's founder, one Charles Lazarus, who apparently liked the lilt of his last name.

1.5
Fascia chaos. It's actually improved here by the structured architecture, but the latter is itself not well done. Cars, a row of piglets, nose up.

1.6
Strip center façade detail overload: the next step up from Fig.1.5, with superfluous strip and panel decoration cropping up wherever possible.

in different planes, orientations, materials and details – in short, making things look a bit more like a building group than a strip building hiding behind a flurry of visual incident. However, things will invariably cost more that way, and that's why that sort of thing is mainly seen in relatively nicer places like those resort centers. I'm sorry.

None of the above observations have ventured into the interiors of these centers, but a few things may be said. Shops in older centers will have a front wall largely of glass, permitting views in of the merchandise, views out (though little of merit may be seen), and the admission of a bit of daylight. More recent shops have cut down on the glass--perhaps for security concerns, to afford even more internal periphery for staging merchandise, or just because it's cheaper. Even in the all-glass cases, natural light will play a small part in the internal illumination, which is provided by fluorescent troffers or, in more recent installations, LED downlights, both in a variety of color temperatures depending on whatever got put in when the last one burned out. (Well, LEDs are supposed to almost never burn out, so the gay variety of color temps is harder to explain in those cases.) In more recent interiors, the corrugated deck, bar joists, and ductwork are likely to be visible for all to see, probably painted white, the troublesome lay-in ceilings that always showed the leak stains having been banished along with whatever limited acoustic benefit they afforded (Fig. 1.7).

The alluded-to leaks will have been due to a nearly level roof overhead, featuring a membrane that will, sooner or later, reach the end of its warranty. Levelish roofs are the all-but-absolute rule in shopping centers; don't let those mansard rooflets fool you. Flat roofs are easy to frame and afford a platform for heat and air package units that sit up there in the weather, the ducts coming down and up through *holes in the roof*. This is far and away the rule for HVAC in such places, because it's cheaper, at least for the time being. Retail boxes that are big but not really, really big often resort to gutters and downspouts on the "back" side, the entire roof sloping very gently in that direction. Levelish roofs with a parapet around all the edges are synonymous with bathtubs, and will leak, sooner or later. My, my, all those drawbacks may make one wonder why pitched roofs aren't more common in these cases, but in the event that happens, it would be hard to put package units up there, plus, with these mega-footprints, they will either get absurdly tall or have a slew of valleys having their own water-management problems. Like parking in the front, flat roofs are hard to stamp out.

1.7
Office buildings also often feature the plague of missing ceilings. It bears noting that when conditions overhead have been carefully laid out and simplified, including heating and cooling that doesn't involve forced-air ductwork, they can actually be presentable.

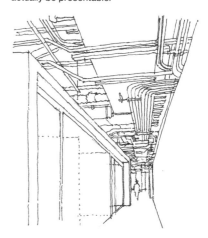

Everyday Architecture: A Vast Wasteland?

1.8
Walgreens: one of the big fake gables versions.

1b.
Drugstores

Since early in the last century, drugstores have sold a lot more than drugs. Nowadays, while the pharmacy in the back is indeed the source of the majority of their profits, there is a lot of business in over-the-counter nostrums, beauty products, greeting cards, photo finishing (is that still really a thing?), and general stuff such as Kleenex, toys, lightbulbs, and goodness knows what all. Plus, a wide variety of snack foods and drinks, including beer, the latter being a pretty ironic complement to the wares of the pharmacy. In this regard, the drugstore is more like a legitimized version of a gas station convenience store. There's one local drugstore around here that had a popular lunch counter for 70 years (though sadly no more), and another that was designed to recall the good old days of the soda counter.[3] But those are exceptions to the rule nowadays, and the rule is Walgreens and CVS.

There are others, but these are the king and the other king of chain pharmacies. Following on its origins at the beginning of the last century, Walgreens went on to sport some handsome Art Deco and mid-century modern stores. More recently, while their stores are sometimes cut to fit an idiosyncratic downtown site, in the burbs they usually feature big square footprints with a cut-off corner for the front doors. That's a clever scheme assuming the store faces a street corner, which it often does but sometimes doesn't. One recalls earlier attempts to decorate the otherwise long and nearly blank sidewalls, such as Walgreens' heavy-duty Dryvit-cladfaux gables, meant perhaps to evoke a homey vibe but instead seeming clumsy and a bit oddly foreboding (Fig. 1.8). CVS had and maybe still has a sort of civic-grandeur effort going on with its Dryvit arch-truss over its cut-off entrance, perhaps as an attempt to distance itself from the Walgreens stores that theirs so thoroughly resemble. Walgreens in turn has focused its front corner on a sacred vitrine for its logo (Fig. 1.9). While both stores do include windows that reach partway back along the sidewalls, they're invariably of the high sill type; one assumes both for security and to preserve a maximum of marketing perimeter on the inside.

Well, that hodge-podge of descriptions aptly reflects the hodge-podge of efforts over the years on the part of these Rx titans to make their stand-alone stores look approachable and pleasant and reliable, efforts that have yet to succeed very widely. Critics have taken these guys to task for their

---

3   Those sodas and floats were probably just as calorie intensive in the good old days as today's corn syrup drinks, which pack 10 teaspoons of sugar-equivalent per 12 ounces of carbonated water. And the "standard" plastic bottle's contents have been 20 oz. for quite a while. Think for a moment about adding 10 teaspoons of sugar to your coffee or breakfast cereal.

All About
Sales

1.9
CVS with arch,
WG with vitrine.

markedly non-pedestrian-friendly exteriors, and indeed that's what they appear to be. Just having the parking lot wrapping both of those "public" faces and more, in the standard way of suburban commercial site planning, automatically signals that this is an establishment for drivers rather than pedestrians (Fig. 1.10). A pedestrian wandering along the perfunctory sidewalk (should there be one at all) alongside the adjoining suburban five-lane connector road will be looked at askance — what is he doing out there? — so it's almost naive to expect the store to provide canopies and colonnades and inviting park benches.

The odd thing is that colonnades and awnings do appear here and there on a variety of Walgreens and CVS outlets across the country, but these amenities have the feel of being add-ons to the basic long, flat sidewall rather than being somehow integral to the design. Is this some kind of duke-it-out situation between modernism and new-urbanist-traditional, transpiring with neither approach having emerged the victor? Ultimately the design players will have been the corporation with its evolving design standards, and whatever the local architect chooses to try to do with them, and neither one is likely to be very invested in setting a new standard for approachable and agreeable design. I'm sorry to report that drugstores turn out to be not very interesting architecturally, which is not so surprising for a place where you go for your Xanax refills and not so much else. A more inviting and open concept would serve the chains well, of course, but for now they seem to be feeding on each other's not-so-inviting and bunker-like schemes for customer hunting in the burbs.

1.10
Suburban WG
in sea of parking.

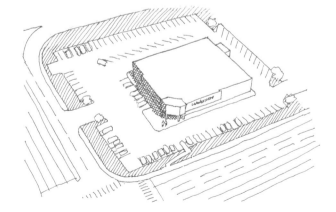

1c.
Assorted Stand-Alone Purveyors

Is there a category for such places? These are the many, many retailer box buildings that have, for whatever reason, not ended up as part of a shopping center or a mall (though many of them are indeed found there also). Let's say they fall into the rough general categories of food and drink, goods, and services:

Food and drink:	• Supermarkets • Bakeries • Juice bars	• Smoothies • Ice Cream • Cookies	• Cakes • Pies • Donuts	• Coffee • Liquor & Wine
Goods:	• Clothing (subtypes) • Five & Dime	• Appliances • Furniture • Paint	• Office supplies • Phones • Vitamins, etc.	• Hardware • Housewares • Crafts
Services:	• Salons • Cleaners • Laundromats	• Tattoo Parlors • Pawn Shops • Tech & Repair	• Palmistry • Massage • Adult Stores	• Rentals • Pet Supplies

What's to be gleaned from this doubtless incomplete list? Some are broadly single-category, supermarkets being about "food, etc.," with butchers and other food subtypes being found therein, though occasionally those also appear as stand-alones, as they did in the "good old days." The line has been drawn here at professional services, meaning doctors, lawyers, and more, who usually find themselves in the different categories of office buildings or clinics.

Aside from supermarkets, food and drink vendors appear to deal primarily in self-indulgence (juice imbibers perhaps believing their indulgence is of a healthful sort). And goods and services seem not infrequently to deal in the generally ill-advised (supplements, tattoos, pawn, palmists, adult stores, massage — though in fairness one should distinguish between "massage" and massage, a legitimate service). You say there's no roadside palmist where you live? Look again.

The only architecture-related conclusion to be reached about this broad cohort would be that, as a rule, their buildings tend to be mightily unmemorable (Fig. 1.11). Occasionally, though, a cleaner's or a bakery or some other long-standing

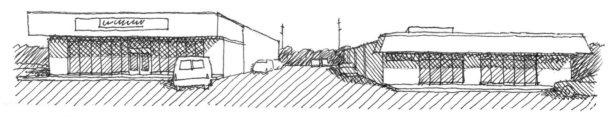

1.11
Some mighty unmemorable stand-alones.

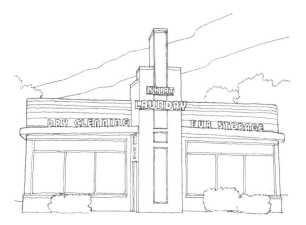

1.12
A thankfully surviving streamline modern stand-alone.

neighborhood purveyor will still sport a nice sign from days long ago when signage was an art as well as a craft, and hints of Art Deco or Streamline Moderne may similarly have survived to the present day (Fig. 1.12). More recent attempts to revive a bit of architectural *joie de vivre* for such places haven't, as a rule, turned out that well, perhaps because such isolated little buildings really don't have much of a context to relate to, so it's hard to find them a convincing identity. Or perhaps because designers as a group have forgotten or never knew these skills.

The internet provides a look, admittedly a superficial one, into what seem to be the trends, if any, in the architecture of such places. Smoothie and juice bar purveyors tend to work with "fresh" colors and simple forms, perhaps in homage to the sometimes fresh products on offer-- at least they have a bit of a theme to start with. At the other end of the scale, supermarkets, usually big, flat-roofed, unwindowed barns, remain prey to the difficult and usually failed problem of decorating the shed; Krogers are often decorated with variations on a ubiquitous appliqued gable. Furniture emporiums have taken that up as well, sticking architectural portal shapes in front with abandon.[4] Often enough these frontal items are all but lost in the endless expanses of 400-foot façades (Fig. 1.13). Ultimately, as with drug stores, for many of these stand-alones, the architecture is the result of corporate design standards, designed to fit anywhere (or nowhere).

We do find that in years gone by, donut shops, cleaners, coffee shops, and the like did some

---

4 Actually, such appliqued front pieces are to be found everywhere, cropping up on fast food outlets, restaurants, clinics, shopping centers – they've become a veritable signifier of everyday architecture. These little temples with their gabled, corniced, pyramided, or arched profiles are trying their best to distract us from the boxiness behind.

1.13
Superlong stand-alones: furniture megastore; supermarket.

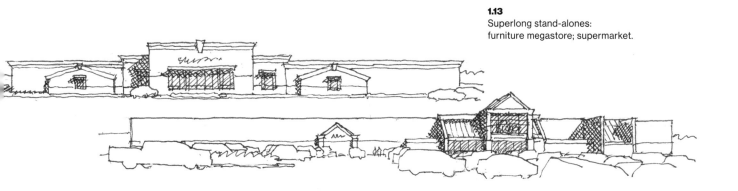

nice things design-wise with skyline signage, or with rakish roof profiles. Weigel's, a modest southern chain best known for milk, coffee, and donuts, originally sported stylish cantilevered shed and butterfly roofs on its little drive-by stores (Fig.1.14). Most of these have since morphed into gas station/convenience stores, their roofs having been sadly eclipsed by the usual flat-roofed nonentities. Perhaps readers are reminded of similar ubiquitous dumbing-down in their necks of the woods.

When it comes to dime stores, few remain. By and large, they are nostalgically recalled things of the past, Woolworth's having gone bankrupt in 1997. Kress stores are also long gone, though many of their handsome Art Deco terra cotta façades still exist, reminders of better days. Mainstays of Main Street, dime stores never evolved into stand-alones; sadly, their role as purveyor of all sorts of cheaper items has since been parceled out to cheaper places such as drugstores, gas stations, and dollar stores.

Other sorts of stand-alones

There are a couple more categories of freestanding one-purpose buildings that crop up in most every city and town, but they aren't marts of trade, nor do they belong in any of the other of these everyday categories. One is light industry. To be sure, some such places need to be next to the railroad, or are noisy or smell bad or have a lot of truck traffic and, in regards to those, it's the right thing to do to have them zoned apart from residential areas (see also "Industry"). But such entities are or would be reasonably good neighbors and serve to vary the urban landscape in a desirable way. What we have instead are whole ghettos of pre-engineered metal buildings, often evincing modest efforts at best to have put some kind of brave front on. In the bigger cities, such a ghetto can be as big as a small town, the very impact of such a density of light industry inevitably drawing down the property values of adjoining residential areas.

The other one is self-storage. It's ironic that these projects sometimes don't look all that bad out there along the stripscape, unencumbered as they are by gaudy signage or much in the way of parking lots. True, they have very little need for windows, though some windows show up anyway in the more deluxe installations to illuminate interior hallways, and one supposes we should be glad to have those. But in truth, the façades of most of these places are largely solid and blank, which does them no favors appearance wise as features of the burbs. Surely speculation that extralegal materials and activities occasionally seek the anonymity of such places is merely fanciful. Anyway, the whole thing of self-storage has to do with elements of the urban landscape that are essentially dead: ossuaries of stuff for people whose McMansions just aren't big enough to house it all. It's a little too bad that this odd building type, the stuff of mausoleums, seems to have become so common: as with parking structures, there won't be a very good way to repurpose them once they are less in demand.

1.14
Weigels: their original butterfly.

1.15
Not that big:
a dollar store.

1d.
Big Boxes

Big Boxes are so named for being bigger than the other boxes: they're the biggest sales emporiums available for walk-in purchasing. Some may be attached to other boxes in shopping centers, or they may be all alone back there behind the also big parking lot. They're single stories of up to 200,000 square feet, or over three football fields in area.

    Some not-all-that-big boxes, reliably found in the more challenged parts of every town, are of the Dollar persuasion: Dollar General, Dollar Tree, Dollar Plus, Family Dollar, and Dollarama. There are more than 34,000 Dollar stores in the United States, more than all the Walmart, Starbucks, and McDonald's businesses combined. They prevail where crime rates are higher, where residents have higher rates of obesity and smoking, and where they have lower levels of education and income. (One doesn't mean to cast aspersions; sadly, facts are facts.) Most are freestanding, and while some can be presentable enough architecturally, more typically the exteriors tend to exemplify archispeak's "decorated shed," with a higher grade of concrete block and a false-front ribbed metal fascia in front, and lesser grades at the sides and rear where the profile of the pre-engineered box is revealed (Fig. 1.15). The false front fooled no one, though no one noticed anyway.

    The kings of Big Boxes are the general merchandise places that sell pretty much everything, and their emperor is Walmart. The author recalls a trade publication article from some time ago wherein an architectural firm that had a grip on a lot of Walmart work stated that, while their work is not especially respected, they really

1.16
Big: a Walmart.

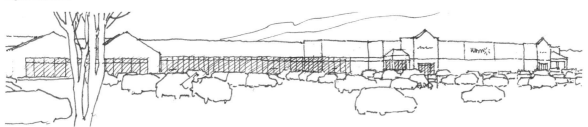

don't care. Walmart itself tended to share that sort of view for some time, although its architectural act has improved slightly in recent years. One experiment has involved concealing its very big box behind a streetwall, its entrance flanked by other much smaller businesses. But in general, the boxes are very large, very uninteresting, and dedicated to serving the shopping needs of those who barely escape the dollar store segment. (Fig.1.16).

Target, a Big Box that actually has ceilings, likewise seems a step up in the quality of its products (and, one assumes, its prices). One detects the hand of an industrial designer here and there in Target properties. Some time back they even featured a line of products designed by noted architect Michael Graves, and while more recent lines fail to measure up to that standard, at least a few nice-looking knock-off items can sometimes be found among the lesser offerings at "Tarzhay."

A further step up in quality and price finds the department stores, or at least you used to be able to find them. Not themselves actually considered Big Boxes for some reason, department stores are in perilous shape due to the ascendence of the BBs and, foremost, the ascendance of [It which shall not be named], the emperor of online shopping and shipping. This huge entity, visible to the consumer primarily as an all-too-easy-to-use site on the internet, encompasses the biggest boxes of all, 185 of them and counting, each four times the size of the biggest Walmart (Fig. 1.17). Buildings at such scales transcend the normal status of architecture and become manmade mesas extending for hundreds of yards, over there past the hundreds of trucks. These "fulfillment centers" have been notorious for the way their employees have been treated like robots, with unreasonable performance goals, thus wage slaves in the truest sense of the word. The company's business plan also includes sending thousands of planes and trucks in all directions, all of the time. It's true that if [It] did not exist, online consuming would remain in some form or other, complete with similar environmental negatives, a putting of that genie back in the bottle being mighty unlikely.

Say what you will about Barnes and Noble, a "retail bookseller Big Box store," but it's sometimes the only bookstore in town and we have to give them that. When the B&N around here was new, it had a whole section of architecture books up there near the front, but that was before the ascendence of the internet, and of [It]. Thereafter, the architecture section shrank to a few shelves in the back. More recently, the author found it comprising all of five titles hidden amongst the arts and crafts. And yet the place is still relatively full of books. It's hard to put a finger on what has filled the gaps left by more substantial fare that is no longer on bricks-and-mortar offer, but it's notable that seven out of the top 20 recent B&N sellers were either of the "Chainsaw Man" or "Jujutsu Kaisen" series, both manga comics. Well at least it's another big box that actually has a ceiling.

One doesn't really think of Home Depots or Lowes's as hardware stores, but that is their main mission, albeit greatly expanded in scope. The dimensional lumber on offer is a sad vestige of the quality one used to get at the local builder's supply, a sort of place that is itself harder to find nowadays, possibly due to the proliferation of Home Depots and Lowes's. Virtually identical, the two depend on homeowners' unwise compulsion to save money by trying to do things themselves. And as with other Big Boxes, their architecture is remarkably unremarkable, aside from the spectacle of customers exiting the front doors pushing carts laden with the likes of whole kitchen cabinets, sliding glass doors, and bathtubs.

As with online Big Boxes, the brick-and-mortar ones are not without fault when it comes to their effects on the economy, the culture, and the environment. In addition to occupying a large footprint and requiring acres of parking, their site development neglects pedestrian or community amenities. They dominate markets while providing no unique culture, products or identity, and require large sales volumes that take sales away from existing retailers. So, it appears that the lack of anything notable about their architecture is just the beginning of troublesome issues when it comes to Big Boxes.

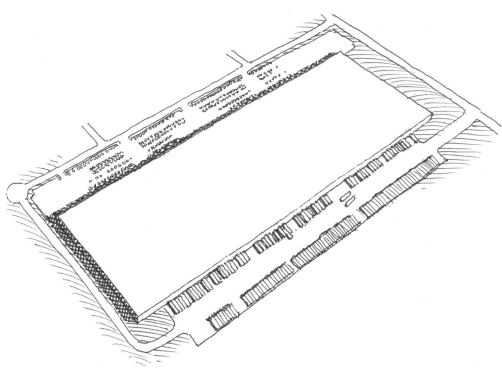

1.17
Biggest: a "distribution center." Note for scale the 18-wheeler truck bodies in front.

dining & other amusements

In part, we amuse ourselves to distract ourselves from that world of commerce. Some amusements are indeed about entertainment, but a lot of shopping itself amounts to amusement, and the same can be said for much of dining out. Sadly, sometimes the designed and built places where these amusements take place end up doing some distracting as well, but in a not so good way.

g
her
ments

002

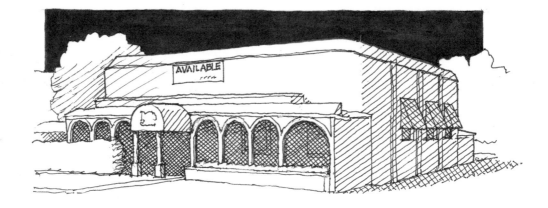

2.1
"Available:" Since demolished.

2a.
Restaurants, Bars, and Breweries

Good restaurant architecture turns out to be oddly hard to define as such. Not long ago, a local favorite closed because the owners decided they had become too old to keep it going. On the outside one could discern, barely, the bones of a shabbily stylish roadside eatery from long ago (Fig. 2.1), and an appraising eye could find much to criticize on the inside as well. One might offer that a fine menu was its saving grace, or that the loyal and friendly staff was exceptional, but there was yet more to it. The rather too small wooden booths enforced a congenial intimacy, as did the two little curtained mini-rooms in the corners, along with warm colors and finishes, a big mirror, and subdued but not too subdued lighting. All were elements of interior happenstance that helped contribute to a pleasurable dining experience. Hard to define, indeed, and to be sure, architecture is but a part of the equation, but it does have a crucial part to play in such one-off dining establishments, for better or worse.

One-of-a-kind restaurants often share one characteristic that chains often do not: inadequate acoustic mitigation. Whether this is due to a pressed tin ceiling or to the fashionable lack of a ceiling, the outcome is the same. One is forced to conclude that the resulting din is misperceived as a signature of popularity; that we are in the right place with the right people, so we are all having a good time talking louder and louder to be heard because everyone else is doing the same. (That's even a thing technically, something called the "Lombard Effect.") It's true, though, that the management at such places sometimes have second thoughts as a result, evidenced by added-on panels of foam or of something or other to be seen or found on the deck or the walls or the undersides of the tables and chairs. Generally, these are not going to help very much, for better acoustically absorptive products are what's needed, and in larger areas. But acoustic ceiling panels are evidently seen as outmoded, since it appears that we prefer to see the ducts and wires and bar joists and corrugated deck and concrete, paying homage to the fact that we're tough and we don't need any mollycoddling, we're urban and urbane and love the ugly, unfinished nature that much of urban redevelopment now seems to entail (Fig. 2.2).

2.2
Industrial chic.

Dining & Other Amusements

Or something like that; the ultimate motivation seems hard to pin down. There's "let's play house in this old garage"; indeed, maybe it harks all the way back to childhood, hunkering in packing crates or under a card table with a sheet over it. And it may play into a parallel motivation on the part of the developer to spend as little as possible on a new venture, for it can sometimes seem that little more than a coat of paint and a building permit were involved. Well, there is the grease trap, potentially a deal killer for any such business expecting to deal with grease in the menu, which most will. The general trend to faddishly dingy may, in interior design terms, date back to the decline of heavy industry, with big old mills and warehouses newly empty and available for relatively inexpensive adaptive reuse. It was what developers eventually did, and the designers and the public followed suit with buy-in. (That is not to gainsay the fact that some such empty mill buildings took a very long time to get repurposed, or the fact that some such renovations were indeed very well done and far from inexpensive.)

And then there are the chains: Hard Rock Café, TGI Fridays, Texas Roadhouse, Red Lobster, Chili's, Applebee's, Cracker Barrel, Olive Garden, Outback Steakhouse, Cheesecake Factory, and the rest, those said to be among the 25 most popular chain restaurants (Fig. 2.3). One feels a little queasy after such a list, perhaps needing an Alka-Seltzer. Architecturally their recent fates are similar to those of other stand-alone outfits, regarding the general adoption of an efficient rectangular solid with an armory of embellishments brought to bear to distract some attention from this fact. Also likewise, a polite and slightly overstuffed modernism prevails, somewhat emulating the customers in those regards. Specialized chains do have their variants—a shingled Red Lobster, a rubbly Olive Garden, a tin-roofed Roadhouse—some being more successful than others in their thematic scenography, a significant aspect of architecture being, after all, about *mise en scène*.

Beyond such furbelows, though, the architecture of the chains arises from standardized designs produced with no knowledge of an ultimate site, the results thus being relentlessly generic and object-centered, contributing to a nationwide suburban site planning default of boxes in rows that demean exterior space instead of defining it. Among the chains, Cracker Barrel gets some sort of venture planning prize for its cheap frame boxes that actually look pretty good, its store full of things no one needs that one must struggle through on entry or exit, and its unchallenging menu of comfort food. Working fireplaces! Generously scaled restrooms! They're so popular

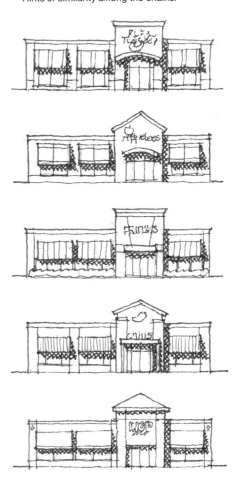

2.3
Hints of similarity among the chains.

that they can be and are sited on leftover plots back behind everything else because their people know how to look for and find them.

"Diners" are somewhat different from dining and fast-food chains. Well, it seems there actually is a category of chains called diners, including the likes of IHOP, Waffle House, Denny's, and Shoney's, but our subject is the actual thing called diners. They've had a notable history of providing quick, sometimes questionable fare in sometimes memorable little buildings that had their origins in railroad dining cars (Fig. 2.4). From the '20s to the '40s, many of these were prefabricated and delivered to the site, like mobile homes. While more recent installations have been site-built, they emulate these narrow stainless-clad cafes, their uniquely American milieu having been celebrated in movies and paintings. Diners can be pretty cool: when their efficient profiles and snazzy décor crop up, they afford a refreshing contrast to the chains.

Bars and Breweries

There are bars and there are Bars. There are places like the Bemelmans Bar or the King Cole in Manhattan, and there are places that are repellent and dangerous. Until relatively recently, bars in this country were, as a rule, dark (which remains the norm in semi-rural locales). They seemed to partake of a puritanical view that their patronage was something of a shameful matter to be hidden in the shadows, and indeed it often was and was, with solid exteriors featuring little more than a flotilla of neon beer signs in the window, should there be any windows. Or perhaps, at least in some cases, they were built in dry counties and trying to keep a low profile. By contrast, pubs in the United Kingdom tend to be well illuminated and to be comfortably – sometimes splendidly – decorated. To all appearances, patronizing them was and is a normal part of everyday life, with the whole family stopping off together for a meal, though this is not to imply that pub culture was or is enduringly salubrious in all respects.

As with restaurants, bars and breweries have seized in more recent decades upon the "industrial aesthetic." This works well when there is more enthusiasm than asset brought to a prospective new venture, though when it comes to breweries there is that complicated apparatus of tuns and tanks that must be dealt with. Despite that expense, startup "craft" breweries have become rather thick on the ground, and one is obliged to conclude that they are either overbuilt for the market, or serve to meet a heretofore ill-met demand for lots of beer in communal places.[5] The ductwork, exposed electrical conduits, and concrete slab floors, along with the brick or concrete block walls (perhaps with fragments of the earlier plaster still adhering in places) all contribute to the spirit of rustic bonhomie, as if in a squat in bombed-out Berlin or something of the sort. Call it a classist preference, but the more polished aspect of the retro cocktail lounge, with nice finishes and well-planned lighting, has more enduring appeal than these grittier approaches to the watering hole.

---

5 How harmful can beer be, one may ask, for it's only 4 to 6% alcohol by volume or so. But this relative mildness can lead to large amounts of consumption, which leads, along with the poor American diet, to weight gain, along with the other problems that overconsumption of alcohol can lead to. It is, after all, the world's primary drug of choice and one that we have chosen not to ban here, while banning all sorts of others that vary from being harmful to being hardly harmful at all, though there are changes afoot regarding the latter.

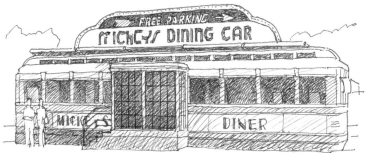

2.4
A diner in St. Paul, MN: stainless steel, baked enamel, neon, three nice fonts.

Dining & Other Amusements

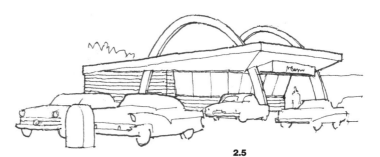

2.5
An early McDonalds.

2b.
Fast Food

The epitome of everyday architecture, fast food emporiums are plentiful along every commercial connector. But dare one say it, the architecture of fast food has gone through an evolutionary process of being dumbed down ever since first arriving on the scene in 1921, which was the year that White Castle began in Wichita, Kansas. McDonald's, the emperor of the fast food industry, didn't get started until 1940, when Mac and Dick McDonald opened their first drive-in in California. Ray Kroc showed up in 1954.[6] White Castle's white castellated imagery continues (though indeed somewhat dumbed down) to this day, but the architecture of McDonald's has undergone an evolution, one that is echoed in the industry generally.

2.6
The suburbanized McDonalds.

The early McD's sported a sci-fi vibe during the '50s: soaring parabolas flanked the snappy uptilted roof, with canted control tower glazing wrapping three sides below it. Red and white striped tile completed the cheerfully extroverted design, where dining was walkup and takeout only (Fig. 2.5). The parabolas were instantly recognizable from a distance, a sign without needing to resort to signage (though of course signage was there as well). But in the '60s, perhaps partly as a result of the need to accommodate indoor dining, Kroc reinvented the look: for decades thereafter, a truly uninteresting, vaguely Polynesian roofscape proliferated, complete with downlit floating beamettes (fig. 2.6). Ever-helpful local zoning boards evidently bear some blame for this initiative, the result being a deliberate turning away from those early "circus-y and garish" qualities to something notably more subdued. One might even say something more suburban, which is where these things were: out along the connector on the way to the ranch houses, also subdued and similarly lacking in eye-catching architectural qualities. A crucial signifier of this step in the dumbing down was the fate of the golden arches, which were eliminated from their noble status as skyline signifiers and repurposed side-by-side as a sign-topping M, though one not found in any font.[7]

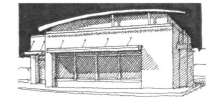

2.7
The boxified McDonalds. The broken off M-leg is trying to convince you that the roof isn't just flat like all the others. In some cases that shape was actually extruded back to create a vaulted roof bay, a clear improvement.

And so, onward to 2011, when McD's made it official that further dumbing down was called for, though it's true that this was not necessarily done in a bad way. This new generation, celebrating the boxiness of modernism by being boxy, essayed an undaring redux of the golden arch in the form of a broken-off golden leg, tipped sideways and perched above the front (Fig. 2.7). Beyond the yellow accents, the color

---

6   He bought the company in 1961, for $2.7 million. After that he began taking credit for its birth.

7   Strangely, not quite true. Googling "McDonald's font" reveals one font and one only, which appears to have been deliberately designed around the swoopy nature of the M, also featuring it upside down as the W. It's a pretty hard-to-read font.

palette tends to be even more carefully browned and grayed, a look said to "project a more refined and grown-up taste" should such a thing be remotely in keeping with the essentially kiddie food on offer.

This evolving fate of McDonalds has been largely shared by their competitors. An Arby's (the name originating with its founders, the **R**affel **B**rothers) was once a distinctive version of a Conestoga wagon along with a big ol' 10-gallon hat sign. But then for some reason the vaulted roof was renovated into a mansardized roofline, and eventually those too were boxified, ending up a whole lot like the McBoxes. Wendy's was basically boxified from the start, being a Johnny-come-lately fast food company that began in 1969, but with mansard-esque fascias that did the box no favors. Their more recent iterations insert a prominent red "blade wall," in the argot of architects, as the signature element in an otherwise lukewarm exercise in modernish wallpapering. Burger King's too-blue roofscape was rather like a simplified version of McD's for many years, BK having also followed the general trend of overall rectangularity in recent times, but with a conservatively *de stiji*-ish vibe.

As for Chick-Fil-A, Dunkin', Domino's, Pizza Hut, Chipotle, Dairy Queen (now emasculated into DQ), Jack in the Box, Popeyes, Whataburger, Hardee's, and most all the rest, you may well know their various idiosyncratic styles of times past, but now they're all boxed up as well. Tasteful, yes, sort of; modernist, yes, in a weak-willed kind of way, with familiar tropes of slightly collided volumes, slightly projecting lids, and slightly cantilevered canopies. It's all a sort of slight triumph for the proponents of modernist architecture with these well-mannered boys lined up along the strip, all taking care not to be too, well, too circus-y and garish, heaven forbid. That said, one suspects in fairness that if they were all gussied up instead in bold, assertive Googie togs, we'd be complaining about that too, about too much of a good thing.[8] Ideally, a mix of the two types – the flashy old modernism and the careful new – would have its merits, but it's in the nature of capitalism, despite its espousal of innovation, that things often end up looking sort of the same instead.

Some other FFs, also rectilinear, also have attributes of note. Some time ago Taco Bell (named for its founder, Glen Bell) started down an arguably wrong path when it took its perfectly ok south-of-the-border hacienda concept and watered it down: th'box was now in the ascendent at th'Bell (Fig. 2.8). Sonic, notably different in nature by virtue of its drive-up "American Graffiti" canopies, has encountered an ironic problem with having gone along and boxed its formerly vaulted central canopy, plus having sharpened up its drive-up canopies: the two alterations, each bravely in the spirit of updated imagery, just don't fit together well like they used to. And while KFC has made some brave experiments here and there with idiosyncratic form-making, by

---

[8] "Googie" is the appropriately raffish-sounding term for "futuristically space-age architecture from back in the day," prominent examples being found in Los Angeles. The original McDonalds are sometimes considered stylistically Googie.

2.8
Taco Bell: the well-formed early version; the lip-service-on-a-box later version. Note the dissonant pairing of two arch profiles on the latter.

Dining & Other Amusements

2.9
Siamese co-branding along the interstate: a blind date of logos and skyline signifiers.

and large the box triumphs here too. KFC's "identity" has undergone some interesting tweaks over the years as well, one being the transparent ruse of acronymizing Kentucky Fried Chicken so that it sounds more, well, more healthful, perhaps. The Colonel himself has had some updating, first having been reduced to a big tilted head with a twinkle in his eye, but then more recently appearing togged in an apron with his expression subtly tweaked into one of bland beneficence. Finally, amidst these cavils, Starbucks deserves a thumbs up for avoiding the boxy trend, with crisp gabled and shed roofs on some of its stand-alone shops.

Of this lot, Panera Bread (not to be confused with Atlanta Bread – and what are we to make of the many similarities between the two, including the name and the logo? Inquiring minds want to know) is a slightly different animal, being of the growing "fast-casual" persuasion, meaning nicer interiors, better quality menus, and higher quality prices. That distinction aside, they've been boxified like the rest, and indeed the FC trend is said to have been an influence in the corresponding general boxification and "tastefulness" direction of the whole FF crowd. So, the FC concept may be regarded as a bit of a trend in an up direction.

But there's also an arguably down direction trend in the industry, or at least its architecture, and that would be the Siamese-ing together of fast food outlets and gas stations – or other fast food outlets – out along the interstate (fig. 2.9). The industry calls this co-branding, and calls the gas stations convenience stores, which is indeed what they have largely become. One can't exactly gainsay the, well, the convenience of having the gas, the food, the restrooms, and the vast junk food resupply opportunities under one roof. But the integrity, to use the term loosely, of the imagery of either conjoined outlet is inevitably somewhat debased thereby, with each understandably wishing to preserve its current look, now right next to a competitor's often very different look.

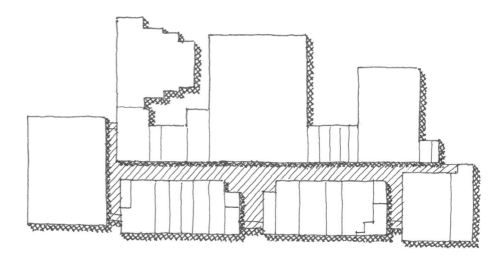

2.10
A typical shopping mall floor plan, here featuring an anchor in the middle as well as at the ends. The cineplex at the upper left has the look of an add-on; such efforts were increasingly made to "diversify" a mall's attractions.

2c.
Shopping Malls

Rightly or wrongly, herewith a made-up distinction between shopping *centers* and shopping *malls.* Evidently, the former can refer to big interior complexes, but herein it's applied to mean an agglomeration of retail boxes with no interior connection (see "Shopping Centers"), while a mall does have climate-controlled connective interiors. It seems the term "mall" originally meant a shady pedestrian walkway in an urban setting and was thus not illogically applied to early shopping complexes of the '50s, which did indeed feature outdoor walkways, possibly with saplings that it was hoped would someday provide shade. Once air conditioning became a perceived necessity of life as we know it, the walkways were roofed over and walled off from the out of doors, but the term remained.

There's a sort-of science to mall layouts. At least two "anchors" are required, at the opposite ends of the pedestrian walkway, i.e., the mall (though the whole thing is now called a mall), for the purpose of magnetically urging us past the smaller stuff in between, though somehow also urging us to patronize the smaller stuff (Fig. 2.10). At least that was once the theory, though nowadays with so much shopping and shipping being done via [It which shall not be named], the anchors have become less magnetic, have changed hands, or have disappeared. Originally the nation's mercantile pride and joy with their phone-book size catalogues of everything—not that a phone-book analogy is meaningful anymore either—department stores were once stand-alone sales emporiums, but they are only remembered nowadays as anchors, or the anchors they once were, having been sadly diminished by the ascendence of big boxes, and by [It]. Back in their heyday, one went to Sears (or someplace else, but it was probably Sears) to buy, let's say, a washer. You looked at the washers, talked to one of the several sales staff, bought it on layaway, had it delivered and installed, and used it for 50 years. Nowadays, Sears and many of its ilk are gone, and instead you Google the matter, try to manfully to assess the various online comments and ratings provided by amateur videographers about the multifarious products available, and perhaps "chat" with someone in Bangalore about your questions. Eventually you reveal your 16-digit credit card number, being ever so slightly concerned that this information thus released will soon be used by international thieves on the dark web, and actually do get it delivered.

The thing is, as most every appliance repairman will tell you, the newer models are not nearly as durable as the older ones, being made in Asia or some other distant place where labor is cheaper, at least for the time being, and of thinner and less durable materials, in order to compete with other companies' products doing the same thing. Or it may be America-built, but to a cheapened standard that can compete with the foreign-born. Perhaps all that seems a bit remote from everyday architecture. Well, the point is that architecture of any kind – "bricks and mortar" – is being rapidly replaced by [It] when it comes to consumer consuming. ("Consumer" is kind of a nasty word when you think about it; we go to these places to consume, to participate in the big American job of getting things and using them up, gobbling them up, now expanded yet further by our obsession with digital things which aren't actually things.)

One could opine that it's sort of pointless to critique the bad architecture of shopping malls if they're all going south, as predictions have it. But that's going to take a long time, and eventually, if the New Urbanists' advice is taken, they'll get reworked and recycled and turned inside out to become better town centers for better towns (Fig. 2.11). Well, that can sound a bit unlikely, but it's a nice idea.

So, when it comes to the possibly doomed shopping malls, what can one say about their physical qualities? The interior walkway is indeed, ultimately, an analog for a shady downtown street, but without the cars and without the weather. Now, that's a pretty nice situation when you think about it, as far as it goes, especially given the often terrible weather we have on this continent,[9] but it's a bit of a dilemma. Lost in the bargain are most of the other wide variety of businesses and institutions that a self-respecting downtown is made up of. To wit, malls lack clinics, branch banks, bars, churches, apartments, post offices, hotels, or learning institutions, among other such entities.[10] It may seem odd to imagine any of these in a shopping mall, but why is that, actually? Perhaps we don't miss them because they were never there; after all, malls were always supposed to be just about shopping. Indeed, a mall is really just one thing, managed by some far away corporation and located far away from downtown in a place that's all but utterly unreachable by pedestrians. True, there are a bunch of pieces of the one thing, being retailers or food sellers, as well as (sometimes) cinemas or drug stores, but by and large malls are just big retail emporiums: palaces of consumerism. Well, again, surely that was the idea, but still, it hardly seems enough for a well-balanced diet of what poses as an "alternative city center." To be more accurate, such posing was not intentional: malls became such things – kind of inadequate community center places – as ironic replacements for the multifaceted downtowns which the shopping malls had helped to decimate.

But back to what passes for the architecture. It turns out to be sort of hard to come up with something to say about it because it's not really quite there. On the outside we find all the dumpsters and delivery doors and egress doors and electrical panels and transformers, with various screen walls trying to hide them, sort of. As opposed to the shopping center, which has an entry side and a service side, the outside of the mall is *all* service side (Fig. 2.12). True, there are the entrances leading to the pedestrian ways, plus the anchor store entrances, each flossed up

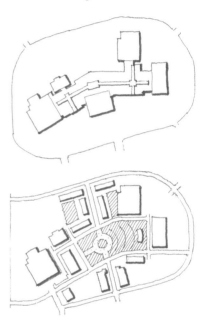

2.11
A proposal for transforming a typical shopping mall (above) into a mixed-use neighborhood center with a park in the middle and parking lots populated with residential buildings.

---

9   Does that sound like an unpatriotic claim in the home of the brave? We have had among the worst hurricanes and tornadoes on earth, plus among the most extensive wildfires and greatest temperature swings. And that was before global warming (excuse me, "climate change") began to usher in the end times that we have caused. Living here does have its undeniable benefits, but these facts remain ever so slightly troubling.

10   It's not a widespread trend, but some of these non-retail elements, such as drop-in clinics, are beginning to appear in shopping malls. And even churches and branch university facilities are appearing in retrofits of "dead" malls.

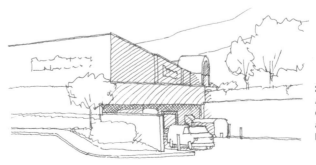

2.12
A shopping mall's outsides: front doors and back doors trying to hide from each other.

2.13
A shopping mall's insides: tall spaces, glass elevator, kinetic sculpture, skylight expanses, potted plants, sweeping balconies, all meant to evoke: what? An imagery of wealth, to be sure, perhaps to help encourage a spending thereof, but more in the nature of "something different." Bigger than life, more elaborate, more exotic, a sort of Disneyland of retail. But the generic glamour of these places is ultimately neither exotic nor ingratiating: a glitzy promise of nothing in particular.

with whatever architectonic eye candy is currently fashionable. All this is on view upon one's plodding approach from the parking lot doughnut surrounding the mall. This approach is not mitigated by sidewalks either, or trees, or anything, except possibly in close proximity to the entrances; patrons are obliged, just as at shopping centers, to walk up the asphalt driving lanes, ever alert to oncoming cars or those approaching from behind, it being, after all, their rightful territory. Indeed, much of the typical outside doesn't amount to much when it comes down to it. (Tellingly in this regard, an internet search for images of malls produces only interior views.)

When it comes to said interior views – that is, of the pedestrian ways – such a term seems woefully inadequate what with the splendiferous assortment of vaulted skylights, escalators, potted trees, waterfalls, and much else that adorns the route we must take to the place where we need to get the coffee filters (Fig. 2.13). But we goal-oriented consumers are only one part of the crowd, others being there to mall-walk, or simply to wander around at random, engaged in a sort of consumer porn to be vaguely titillated by the enormity of consumer opportunities and glittering stuff on offer.[11] The pedway segments tend to be longish because they are defined by the retail frontages that we are supposed to be walking past and, the system hopes, also distracted and entranced by. And it is "designed" in some way or other. What is the correct architectural imagery for the interior of a shopping mall? There isn't one, really, and this leads to any amount of effort of coming up with a "look"; something a step up from gypboard fascias and lay-in ceilings, and we all agree that something of a step up from that is very much needed, but what?

A logical choice might be a return to first principles, treating the pedway as if it were a pedestrianized downtown streetscape: a judicious simulation of being outdoors, with durable but attractive pavements, street trees, lampposts, variegated retail frontages, and perhaps some sort of ingenious simulated skyscape overhead. The theme does have its merits; carried further – and these have all been done – it could feature a bandstand, a clock tower, a town square, a picnic shelter, a playground, a fairground midway. I magnanimously offer this perfectly suitable concept at no cost to anyone wishing to take it on and to figure out how on earth the ceiling treatment would work.

A fairground midway? The author once worked on a mall in the Midwest centered on a big-top tensile membrane tent over an entertainment center based on midway precedents (Fig. 2.14). (It was built, but things have a way of changing, and the idea of a midway as a focal point was a bit of a fad of those times thirty years ago. Google reveals the whole space is now consumed by a Bass Pro Shop. Oh, well...) The author also once worked on a concept design for a huge regional mall in the northeast that was to be themed according to old-world architecture and urbanism: one section Bavarian, another

---

11 The walkers and wanderers will generally be garbed in sweatpants, slogan-emblazoned T-shirts, and $250 running shoes seemingly made of a variety of glued-together scraps. A debasement both of the meaning of "casual" and of pride in one's appearance, something like this holds true at many of those other everyday places as well.

Dining & Other Amusements

2.14
Big top retail
in Clarksville, IN.

Parisian, others London- or Casablanca-inspired, plus a whole skylit, courtyard-centered wing kitted out like a Venetian piazza, complete with canals (Fig. 2.15). That last part now seems rather small potatoes what with the Venetian casinos in Vegas and Macau. It felt just a little cheesy to be working on it, and indeed nothing ultimately came of it, and that's probably a good thing. But at least in these two cases there were guiding themes. Again, more often than not there isn't one, and what we often see instead is a half-hearted attempt to boost the magnificence of the interior in one vague way or another. Mirror-finish materials may be involved. Classical elements are also likely. Ultimately the reality of the mall seems to be one of a retail-themed theme park, a place out of time and removed from the realities of daily life, where we can be vaguely amused, pass the time, have a poor lunch, and possibly buy some stuff we don't really need.

2.15
Venetian retail
in Providence, RI.

2.16
A suburban multiplex: some can afford flamboyant entry marquees, but many are like this one, powerless to transcend the windowless nature of the building type.

2d. Entertainment

"Entertainment" in everyday architectural terms makes up a wildly diverse cohort of building types, but on the outside they're not all that diverse. As with shopping malls, their exteriors tend to be massive, enigmatic, and uninvolving. We are speaking of the likes of movie multiplexes, arcades, bowling lanes, laser tag emporiums, skating rinks, dance halls, and concert halls, all similarly beset with large, solid expanses of exterior wall. True, some effort is made at the entrance, but this often evinces design inexperience and budgetary limitations. Every city is likely to feature all of these hulking around somewhere, typical features of the urban/suburban scene, but features that tend to have a hard time "fitting in."

Speaking of movie houses, their fate over the decades has been a sad story. The original movie houses were often splendid downtown palaces, that remain – those that do remain – treasured center-city anchors. But movie houses in the 'burbs were twinned and then multiplexed in response to irresistible economic forces and competing with at-home moviegoing, resulting in the cheapened little experiences out by the Home Depot that we have today (Fig. 2.16). When it comes to bowling alleys – renamed "lanes" perhaps because actual alleys were rather disreputable, trashy places, as indeed bowling establishments sometimes were as well – they also had a somewhat illustrious design history, with mid-century architecture featuring vaults, parabolas, A-frames, and neon (Fig. 2.17). While modern-day bowling establishments have a hard time emulating those precedents very well, they at least succeed in having a bit of streetscape impact. And when it comes to music halls, while a select few are mightily attention-getting – Walt Disney Concert Hall in LA comes to mind – such places are also more likely to be simply ponderous, with their blank sides and rears doing their settings no favors. They'd probably like to be considered "civic" buildings of a sort, but when it comes down to it, they're really more about entertainment.

Dining & Other Amusements

2.17
From the glory days of bowling center design. In southern California, now demolished.

Some less universally common entertainment-centered facilities would include the likes of casinos, museums, and entertainment centers. (Somehow the term "building" long ago came be regarded as too mundane, many buildings having been upgraded to the status of facilities or centers.) Even at its best, casino architecture evokes a combo of fantasy and transgression, and its more typical incarnations can represent a sort of apogee of tasteless design crapola. Children's museums by their nature tend to be cheerful and innovative architecturally, and we're happy to have them, affording as they do some bright spots amidst the disappointment of which we must generally speak. Some grown-up museums have also been done well, though here as well the general record is less uniformly encouraging (Fig. 2.18). But are museums about entertainment? Broadly, yes, though it's true they are also considered civic buildings.

It's the so-called "family entertainment center" building type, having come about over the last 30 years or so, that epitomizes a multifaceted approach to indoor entertainment. (But beware of Googling in search of examples of entertainment centers, as you will instead be shown where to buy furniture for your flatscreen and speakers.) Chuck E. Cheese and Dave & Busters are two examples, the former being insistently kid-focused and the latter rather more bad boy adult focused. Relentlessly

2.18
A suitably eye-catching children's museum (Chattanooga); a less suitably eye-catching art gallery (Alberta).

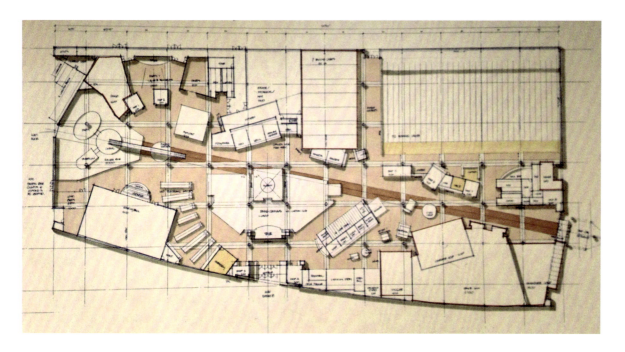

2.19
An entertainment center floor plan, being an unbuilt scheme from the early years of the building type. In a case of planning by aggregation, this client would repeatedly come across some additional type of attraction or game, and space was then made for it one way or another in the constantly evolving plan.

inner-directed, the contents of such places may include arcade games, sports simulators, dining and drinking, miniature golf, roller skating and more (Fig. 2.19). One may question, just a bit, the societal worth of such places, but at least they get people away from their home screens for a while. As with the activity, the architecture is all on the inside at the FEC with a variety of carnivalesque form, color and lighting, while the outsides tend to be more of that solid and hulking sort.

A sort of ultimate in entertainment centers would be the outdoor variety, namely, the theme park. To be sure, these are far from everyday, varying in scale from modest village-like installations to destination mega-attractions. The industry leader is Disney, and deservedly so; just be sure to take twice the money you think you will remotely ever need when you visit. The Disney parks have done such a good job with their main streets and other thematic architecture that their efforts merit study by those doing "legitimate" urban design. And not all such places are out of doors: massive indoor theme parks exist, in the Emirates, Korea, Canada, and the USA, though they tend to be more in the nature of amusement parks than theme parks. It's fair to say that any remnant of "educational" content will have been expunged from the former category, which is primarily about thrill rides.

The biggest structures of all that are dedicated to the entertainment of spectators are, of course, stadiums and arenas. These can be so large, at least in the case of major league scale venues, that it's no longer possible to ignore their physical prominence, and considerable effort can go into giving them special qualities of memorable presence, or at least this seems to be the motive. Design trends for arenas and stadia are notably low on subtlety, ranging from nostalgic borrowings of olde ballpark imagery to extravagant, sometimes rather desperate flights of modernist fantasy featuring flying triangles, whirling cyclones and the like (Fig. 2.20).

Dining & Other Amusements

2.20
Some present-day arenas in Minneapolis and Atlanta, these of the triangles-galore variety.

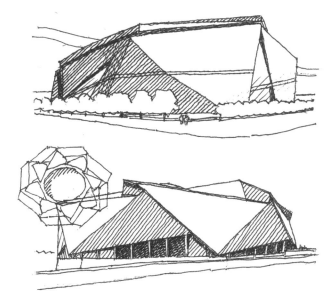

A desirable trend with minor league parks sees them integrated into the urban fabric as opposed to being relegated to farmer's field locations and incorporating elements of commercial and residential development. In this respect they exemplify a worthy effort at fitting in.

Arenas may generally feature those sports events that aren't quite as large-scale as football or baseball (though both now do exist in fully enclosed stadium mega-structures), and they sometimes also feature a unique category called "Sports Entertainment," notably the activities of World Wrestling Entertainment (previously World Wrestling Federation, until the World Wildlife Fund raised an issue with that). Pro boxing, although presumably regarding itself as somewhat more legitimate than pro wrestling, remains a brutal display that can appeal to the baser instincts of spectators. It also constitutes a notable exemplar of one of the main reasons pro sports are so popular, which is sports betting. The author, brushing up on casino and entertainment architecture long ago, came across something enigmatically called "sports book." What could this be: some sort of walk-through version of an encyclopedia dedicated to the history of sport? Sadly of course it means something more like "sports bookie," where you can sit in a big room full of big screens displaying a wide variety of in-progress sports events and place your electronic bets.

institu

...tions

There are some pretty big and pretty long-lasting buildings that serve the institutions of modern society, including the likes of civic buildings, schools, churches, universities, and hospitals. Some banks and businesses would like to be considered civic too, sort of. It's too bad this cohort doesn't do a better job of representing the better side of a community with correspondingly better buildings.

003

3a.
Branch Banks

Branch banks seem more than a bit vestigial nowadays, what with so many transactions taking place in the digital world of the not exactly real. But brick-and-mortar branch banks are still around, and oddly enough still being built, sometimes by Johnny-come-lately outfits such as the 10th 11th bank or the northeastern southwest bank. Collectively branch banks aren't quite as objectionable in architectural terms as some other everyday architecture types, and there are definitely some things of interest, both pro and con, to be pondered.

Long ago, banks were designed to project solidity and security (Fig. 3.1). But at some point, things changed and a sense of friendly accessibility became the norm, or at least the norm to be attempted, and a bank's branches were the main conduit for this effort at make-believe. That trend has continued to the present day, one result being attempts to demolish the perceived standoffishness of the teller line. Originally featuring "teller's cage" grilles, then a glass barrier, and then just a counter, the line is gone altogether in some newer branches, with banking associates (no longer mere tellers) now standing at freestanding stations which the customer sidles up to as if ambling in from the marts of trade to share a tall tavern two-top.

A unique element of branch banking that's had a strong architectural impact has been the drive-through. Branch banks per se having originated in the '20s, the first drive-throughs were pioneered in the USA in the '30s, becoming widely popular by mid-century (Fig. 3.2). In larger such installations of several lanes, each lane had a sleek little kiosk with a sleek little teller inside, right there in the drive-through. And in some cases, reportedly, each had a steep little stair to a secure little tunnel leading under the driveways to and from the bank. We still see money changer personnel in glass boxes at parking garages and turnpikes, but at branch banks, not so much: while they persisted into the '60s, they were rendered obsolete by the pneumatic tube systems we see today. Well, we didn't so much see those at first because they went back to the inside teller underground where all self-respecting outdoor utilities should reside. But, just as with phone lines and power lines and cable lines, they've ended up overhead, snaking around in a nakedly exposed fashion, back to the person behind the bullet-resistant window at the first drive-through lane. And now even that window's gone since, in many cases, that person is too busy manning a two top inside, so it's all about cameras, which we're all not so happy to have still embedded in our lives since we got so sick of them in 2020. And even the drive-throughs, which did ultimately make the branch bank interiors a bit desert-like, have themselves been used less and less due to the ATM, first the walk-up variety and then, naturally, the drive-past variety. And even *those* are being a bit sidelined by the mobile app-iness of online banking.

3.1
Small town bank as anchor of neoclassical stability.

3.2
A branch bank drive-through from 1959.

Institutions

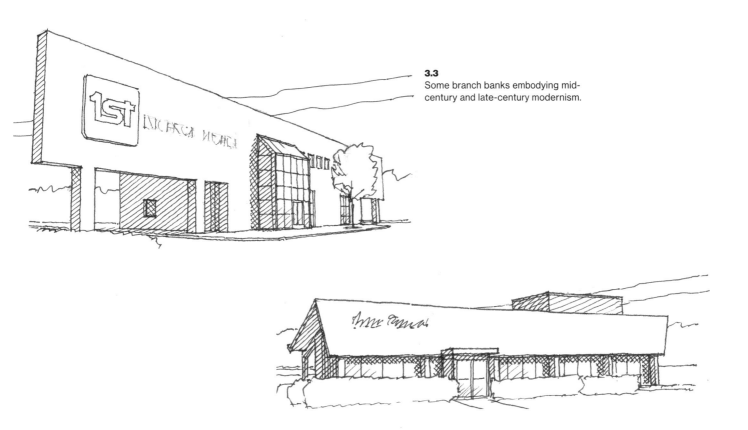

3.3 Some branch banks embodying mid-century and late-century modernism.

Regarding their architectural qualities, some pretty snazzy modernist branch banks made their appearance in the '50s, a setting of trends which some enlightened designers have managed to emulate to this day (Fig. 3.3). But this is not to imply that the average branch bank nowadays is all that snazzy; indeed, it is rather likely to have been suited up in pseudo-Georgian duds. Comments herein under the heading of the "McMansion" regarding columns, pediments, and windows apply here as well; even more pertinently, in fact, as there never were neoclassical precedents for a branch bank. The drive-through is particularly difficult to pull off from an historicist perspective, giving the game away as they tend to do when the roof invariably cantilevers beyond the last pair of columns, themselves generally being too skinny, too far apart, or both (Fig. 3.4). Another sticking point on the branch bank exterior that occasionally appears is a particularly inventive treatment of the keystone: it shows up as usual at the top of a round arched window (arch-topped windows subtly alluding, perhaps, to the virtually sacred place of money in society), but sometimes, apparently of the view that the more is the merrier, also at the *base* of the arch (Fig. 3.5). This odd and deeply wrong use of the keystone shape was probably resorted to when the voussoir brick rimming the arch came to a stopping point and the designer was at a loss as to what should go next, and what a handy economy it must have seemed to use the same precast shape three times per window.

All of which is to say that "traditional" branch bank exteriors of current times, trying to project solidity and security in a sort of weak-willed return to first principles, don't do a very good job of it architecturally. Reasons for this would include the difficulty of translating the historicism of a downtown bank to the suburban reality, but also the apparent

3.4
A Quasi-Georgian branch bank.

difficulty nowadays of getting a confident grasp on an historicist design vocabulary to begin with. The encouraging news is that the rather jazzy modernist work of the '50s is still being done, but the not so good news is that it's just not being done as well now. Somehow the intervening decades, awash in modernist and postmodernist and deconstructivist trends and whatnot, have rinsed away a confident grasp of this as well: of something as simple as a snappy and appealing little branch bank.

Of the rest of the branch interior, beyond the teller line (or the teller stand-up tables), there are the usual suspects: tables with slips to fill out with the pens that don't work, offices for the officers, maybe even a vault! Though the vault is, or used to be, primarily occupied by safe-deposit boxes, and there were those little booths where you could clip your coupons or do other possibly less legal business in private. In that regard, according to a *New York Times* article, the estimated 25 million safe-deposit boxes in America operate in a legal gray zone within the highly regulated banking industry, for the word is that there are no federal laws governing the boxes, and no rules require banks to compensate customers if their property is destroyed or stolen, so fair warning. Anyway, these usual interior suspects may still be there, especially if the branch bank was built thirty years ago, and those branches are also likely to have a lavish amount of interior space that is not being used very intensively in the current app-y age.

In addition to branch banks, there are other suburban financial buildings meant for use by the general public, such as credit union branches. But really, these are very much like branch banks. And there are check cashing outfits, which are simply legally crooked ways to fleece the working poor. One is pleased to have had a tenuously related opportunity to insert that opinion.

3.5
The same bank showcasing its Quasi-Georgian keystones. (Otherwise this is actually not a bad historicist composition.) The repetition of the key-shape works for the round gable vent but not for the windows

Institutions

3b.
Churches

Churches, synagogues, and mosques have been anchors of urban life and form for as long as civilizations have considered themselves civilized,[1] though they (the civilizations) have often been wrong about thinking themselves civilized. Temples are the centerpieces of what we remember and admire about ancient Greek civilizations, and Romanesque or Gothic cathedrals were the undisputed pinnacles of architectural achievement in the Middle Ages – undisputed to this day, a cynical critic might opine. In these modern times in America, even if a town should comprise but three buildings, one is likely to be a church. There's much to find fault with about many modern-day religious edifices, but one essays onto shaky ground if daring to be very specific about such concerns. That said, surely some generalizations are fair enough to make.

An iconic image of the church that is prototypical across the US is the white clapboard chapel, with a modest white steeple integrated into the front façade. Many of these are fine examples of folk architecture, lovingly preserved (Fig. 3.6), though it must also be said that many languish in disrepair due to the relocation or simple dying out of their congregations. The troubling thing about this prototype, as realized in modern times, is its seemingly inevitable debasement. Having proliferated to become far more numerous than their forebears, their steep roofs have become shallow, the arched windows rectangular, the clapboard siding vinyl, and the steeple something from a catalog, or imagined by a handy member, or gone altogether (Fig. 3.7). In somewhat larger versions, the roof's low profile may arise from the building having been a "pre-engineered" one, or may simply reflect a roof structure of gang-nail gable trusses. It doesn't do to blame the parishioners for these bare bones realities, as it may be all they could manage in an age when both dimensional lumber

3.6
White clapboard chapel.

3.7
White clapboard chapel, a modern-day version.

---

1 There are upwards of 3000 mosques, 4000 synagogues, and 350,000 churches in modern day America.

3.8
A megachurch.

and the craft of carpentry have fallen on hard times, as has the expectation of what a suitable house of worship would be like. All that said, one should note that a good many small town and country churches represent good faith efforts, so to speak, often featuring brick veneered exteriors, so all is not lost.

At the opposite extreme in scale from little country chapels we find the megachurches. Some of these have faced up to the reality that their naves are more in the nature of arenas, and have worked effectively within an aesthetic of modern-movement rectangularity as opposed to some dimly recalled ecclesiastical prototype. But the latter case is often the rule, wherein a traditional steeple is flanked by some version of massively overscale extensions, splayed to accommodate the thousand or more that may attend each of the several Sunday services (Fig. 3.8). Many attendees will do so virtually, and those present in person will be served by massive video screens to better convey the parts played by the several ministers, several choirs, and several musical ensembles. The interior is indeed an arena, wired for sound and light, theatrical in spirit and likely to be windowless. Perhaps it's fair enough that the nature of the architecture is wholly secondary to this wholly interior experience, but the megachurch nave seems an ironic recall of the bare bones chapel in this regard, having become a big barn version and often having little intentional architectural expressiveness. On the exterior, an apparent desire for the perceived validation afforded by traditional church design has sometimes resulted in ill-informed appliques of historicist motifs, such as scatterings of pedimented windows and overscale glazed archways.

Strictly to see what would appear, the author made an internet search for "best church buildings in modern America" and one result was a post by "Tripadvisor" – ever the trustworthy research resource – listing "America's 20 Most Beautiful Churches, Cathedrals & Basilicas to Visit." These comprised 19 historicist edifices that were built long ago and one of a modernist persuasion (Sedona's Chapel of the Holy Cross). Such a selection, sobering enough for an unrepentant modernist, reflects a hard reality of religious architecture in modern times: the examples most admired by many are neither modern nor recent. Casting about among everyday cities and their everyday architecture for a handle on what does seem worthy, one does find that a recall of the past is most often present in religious buildings that stand out for their architectural, as well as urbanistic, competence (though it's a bit sad for "competence" to appear as a benchmark). It seems fair to say that brick-clad churches of an historicist persuasion are generally more convincing architecturally than vinyl-clad ones, and that stone-clad ones are more convincing yet. Daring to name a denomination in this regard, one seems on firm ground in praising the Episcopalians for a frequently admirable job in church design and construction, which is, often enough, stone clad. But here again, as is so often the case nowadays, things come down to money, and

Institutions

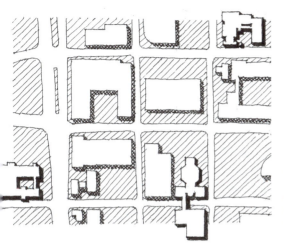

3.9
A view from above highlighting three actual downtown churches, illustrating the positive role that complex church massing can play.

stone is usually the most expensive cladding there is, so brick is more likely to be the best we can hope for.

That reference to "urbanistic" matters concerns the fact that churches are sometimes the only interesting buildings around. Many an otherwise dull town is saved from utter ignominy, at least in terms of the drive-by impression it makes, by the intriguing massing qualities of a church (Fig. 3.9). Churches of a medium to larger persuasion will usually need a battery of Sunday school rooms, an office suite, and a fellowship hall with a commercial kitchen adjoining. Toward the larger end, they may also feature a chapel, parlor, choir rehearsal room, or youth fellowship suite. The fellowship hall may have a stage, and the kindergarten will have an outdoor play space. All of which is to state the obvious, that churches are often, if not usually, multi-building complexes, even though connected under a contiguous roofscape. Some may have felicitously gathered their forces around a cloister court, while others will have simply rambled on as occasion suggested.

While a generally historicist approach to church architecture can be good for the community in this urbanistic sense, a close-up view demands something more, for the apropos saying that God is in the details applies especially well in such cases. (Or was it the devil is in the details? Also, perhaps apropos.) Something resembling Gothic or Romanesque Revival – or, rather less commonly, Spanish Revival or neoclassical – needs careful attention to details and proportion to come off well. And that means scholarship and money, either or both of which may be in short supply. The historicist churches we are more likely to know and to like are likely to date from the earlier decades of the previous century, for both the body of historicist knowledge and the craftsmen to apply it are hard to come by at best in more recent times (Fig. 3.10). There was a substantial period – which still prevails in large degree – during which architects were inculcated with a design taboo regarding historicism, and this has had its impact on new church building design. A particular situation that comes readily to mind concerns the not infrequent need to make additions to historicist church buildings. Sometimes we see modernist additions, and this can be ok if they are handled carefully and deferentially (though that can be a deal killer proviso). But sometimes the addition attempts a middle ground, adopting some historicist

3.10
It can be done, but it isn't cheap (a Presbyterian Church in Nashville, TN, completed in 2009).

3.11
A semi-modern/crypto-historicist addition to an historicist church. Some may say it's sort of ok, but it should have been better.

elements, sort of, but not really, so as not to violate that taboo, or out of inexperience, and this seldom turns out well (Fig. 3.11).

When planning for an all-new church complex comes with a desire on the part of the congregation for something with a sense of the past, of permanence, of a tie to the history of their religious persuasion, there are ways to achieve a design without resorting to full-on historicism, for indeed it is usually likely that the budget will not permit the latter. The approach involves judgement about which elements and their disposition are essential to that impression and which are not. It's a difficult line to draw successfully, so to speak, or so the results we see about us tend to indicate.

Having thus praised careful attention to historicism, one should not in turn neglect the potential of good modernism in church design. For as with historicism, modernism (in whatever guise one wishes to use the term) is equally dependent on good judgment in its execution. Google "modern church design exteriors" and one will find a rogues' gallery of the odd and clumsy, featuring few captivating and confident designs. But it bears noting that here and there amidst everyday suburbia there are modernist churches, generally modest and unassuming, which demonstrate that neither historicism nor flamboyance are prerequisites for expressive and appealing religious architecture (Fig. 3.12).

3.12
Some pretty good modern-day church modernism. Among the tropes: low gables, a-frames, sheds.

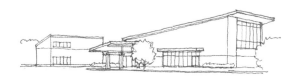

3.13
Art Deco post office (Nashville);
Beaux-Arts branch library (Dallas).

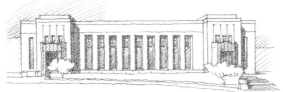

3c. Civic Buildings and "Civic" Buildings

A bit of a catch-all, this category is meant to include such buildings that are more on the everyday than the "monumental" side. Many city halls and county courthouses partake somewhat of the latter, and high-rise versions, regardless of their architectural merits (or lack thereof), may be said to be sort of monumental by definition. This leaves us with lower-rise and not so monumental civic building types, such as branch libraries, post offices, police stations, and fire halls. As opposed to some – perhaps most – of the other everyday building types, these are typified by distinctive and variegated programmatic requirements that potentially lend themselves to expressive and pleasing architecture. Or should. At least post offices can recall a rich history as a type, boasting stripped classical and art deco precedents, some having managed to survive to the present. And branch libraries can look to the admirable heritage of the Carnegie libraries, as well as those by H. H. Richardson and his emulators in the cities here and there that are lucky enough to have them (Fig. 3.13).

But this doesn't mean that more recent works have necessarily learned very much from those forebears. While a review of these types in professional journals shows (sometimes) how well those advantages can be taken advantage of, a corresponding review of internet searches of those same types finds a mishmash of stylistic approaches, often pointlessly striving for dramatic effect, or, equally often, falling flat and missing those opportunities altogether. Many exemplify variants on a common design approach that might be called the "bent cardboard" school of modernism (Fig. 3.14).

There's another building type that isn't quite something you'd call civic, but neither does it fully serve the worlds of commerce, or education, or entertainment. Partaking of all these, it is the convention center, which is indeed sometimes called a civic center. All fair-sized cities have them, their massive footprints often having been elbowed rather rudely into downtown areas to form a sort of symbiosis with downtown hotels, shops, restaurants, and night spots, permitting attendees to conveniently indulge themselves after hours. It's true that given their one-of-a-kind nature they're hardly everyday, and their size has a way of rendering them overbearing

3.14
Some common variants on the bent cardboard school of modernism.

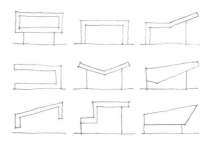

3.15
A pretty good-looking events center (events centers are usually smaller than convention centers, conference centers are smaller yet, banquet halls even smaller).

architecturally unless special pains are taken, though overbearing seems to have been the goal often enough. Efforts are made, however, and one typical architectural treatment involves bringing the smaller, more manageable building elements to the fore and embellishing them architecturally, with the elephant of the big exhibit hall hidden, sort of, in the rear (fig. 3.15).

Schools

School buildings also serve a sort of civic function and are, like the above, distinctive elements in the urban fabric, by virtue of their bulk if nothing else. While public schools were once imposing historicist edifices, since the '30s or so they have generally been more in the nature of dour rectilinear compositions that stretch out across their sites (Fig. 3.16). It's true that large areas of operable glazing or glass block once relieved those expanses, admitting generous amounts of natural light. Natural ventilation was also facilitated when air conditioning was yet in the future, with transoms in the corridor walls further responding to both of these issues. However, much of this common-sense design vanished in more recent times with the several concerns of security, conservation, distraction, or just plain costs, resulting either in the walling over of large glass areas or the simple omission of decent sized windows.

A pervasive floor plan layout for elementary schools features long double-loaded corridors flanked by long rows of classrooms, extending from the "cafetorium" at the entrance end. Some less strait-laced theories of pedagogy have called for smaller pods of classrooms, often with operable walls and shared flex spaces. An ultimate, and somewhat discredited, version of this came about back in the '70s when there was a noisy fashion for the ultimate flexibility of "open classrooms."[2] Along the way, the characteristic rows of desks facing the teacher's desk and blackboard were also liberated, in character with corresponding changes in the very methods of teaching basic subjects, sometimes to the bafflement of parents and some teachers.

The foregoing being essentially about grade schools, what of middle schools? In their floor plan arrangements, they are much the same, except for being larger and having some sorts of gym and, if lucky, music facilities as well. The main difference, however, is not architectural but cultural, many

---

2   There was, and remains in some isolated quarters, a related fad of round dome-roofed building elements, their tumescent volumes slightly recalling flying saucer imagery. These had endemic problems regarding natural light and room proportions. They were sometimes – or were sold as being – useful shelters from tornado weather, so there's that.

3.16
Some typical early- vs mid-20th century public schools, the latter with evidence of covering over much of those pesky windows.

Institutions

3.17
Ivy league CG: Towers, chimneys, stone, variegated openings, and carved surrounds.

students at these ages having transformed into monsters with the onset of puberty (not, to be sure, that grade school didn't also have its share of monsters). The horror of middle school --or in its even more demeaning locution, junior high school-- is well documented and continues unabated, something that architecture is largely powerless to ameliorate.

High schools will be much the same again, though larger yet, the older ones featuring historicist symmetry and a forbidding, never-used main entrance. Here's a case where modernism's off-center compositions and opened-up elevations, along with more welcoming entries and interior common spaces, do favors for the users. Regardless, the main mission of high schools, if one is to judge from appearances, is to play their part in the vast American institution of football, an 11 minute game --well, that's said to be the time the ball is actually in play in NFL games-- well known for its risks of brain damage (meaning for the players, though fans sometimes seem also to be so afflicted). At least football provides an opportunity for music supporters in the form of the marching band, for it facilitates the off-season existence of the concert band, an entity actually concerned with music as opposed to paramilitary close order drill. These issues may seem peripheral to those of public school architecture, but team sports impose substantial physical footprints. Indeed, these have evolved in turn into the biggest structures of all when it comes to university campuses, being the stadiums and arenas, where teams are led by the highest paid university staffers of all, the coaches.

Colleges and Universities

Delving very deeply into college and university architecture seems a bit too much of a step away from the world of everyday architecture, but a couple of pervasive aspects of university planning and design do merit a mention, issues so general and prevalent that they are indeed sort of everyday by definition. One is the enduring appeal of styles from the past on campuses, perhaps most notably in the form of so-called "Collegiate Gothic." One would normally assume that such styles are out of bounds for modernist architects due to those styles' dependence on historicism in design, which we may recall is simply not allowed in most modern-day architecture curricula, sort of like gin before lunch. That's a shame, because Collegiate Gothic (CG) speaks of permanence, history, warmth, and detail. Indeed, it looks good at Duke, Yale, Princeton, and other such elite places, where robber baron patriarchs funded the best in craftsmanship and design (Fig 3.17). Some land grant universities have jumped on the bandwagon, desiring a borrowed sense of ivy-covered respectability, and erected lite versions of CG, the result sometimes being rather thin and unconvincing (Fig. 3.18). As noted in the discussions herein of single-family houses, it's the unaffordability of fine materials and elaborate detail, the lack of able old-world craftsmen, and the lack of historicist knowledge and experience nowadays that are collectively at fault here.

3.18
Knock-off CG: Pointed arches often avoided due to their giveaway that the taboo has indeed been crossed (and that they cost more). Brick throughout, thin gable end walls with ill-proportioned legs, windows in unvariegated arrangements, narrow or no stone surrounds.

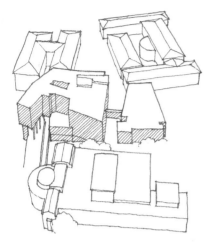

3.19
Brazen disrespect adjoins half-hearted historicism at Pittsburgh's Carnegie Mellon University

Which leads to a corresponding problem on campus when modernism gets mixed in with historicism. On a theoretical level this is well and good, variety being the spice of life and all, and CG being largely unable to be convincingly done anymore anyway, but in reality, such a collegial rubbing of elbows seems hard to pull off. And further to the point, it seems we are in an age when even half-hearted attempts to respect preexisting historicist styles are being elbowed aside by brash efforts of faddish display that respect nothing nearby, new or old (Fig. 3.19).

On such campuses, buildings that are more freestanding seem to fare better, on the face of it, if for no other reason than they are partially freed from such issues of ensemble cohesion. But they have their own problems, residing in that very stand-alone nature. The Oxbridge precedents for such ivy league places had to do with continuity: with buildings as well-defined perimeters for the outdoor rooms of the campus. This is the exact opposite of a freestanding object-building set in the middle of its site, the remaining outdoor space gone more or less to waste around the edges (Fig. 3.20). And the object-building approach is baked into the bones of many modernists.

Offices

Office buildings are not really civic buildings, but they want to be. They can aspire to a gravitas that they don't quite deserve, as in the ubiquitous suburban office "park." Not the high-rise attention-getters, these buildings are the lower-rise realms of professionals, realtors, and financial outfits. As for their external architecture, assorted modernist changes, centering on fenestration, have been rung and rung again over the decades: horizontal stripe windows, vertical slot windows, stacks of rows of vertical slot windows or of square windows ("punched openings" in archispeak), layer cake combos of "colonnaded" ground floors with levels of stripes above (Fig. 3.21). Special elements have been called upon to distract from the repetitiveness of façades that, after all, clad some all but utterly undifferentiated interiors: tweaked corners, notches, steps, bulging entrance bays, and assorted materials superimposed as if they were layered overshirts. Craftsman-ish hipped roofscapes sometimes try manfully to channel a frisson of residential *je ne sais quoi* (Fig. 3.22). To some degree, all these devices have been brought to bear to deal with such largely rectilinear and undifferentiated buildings because architects and developers, as with churches and houses, no longer have proper access to historicist design resources, nor of course do they generally care to. But in the last analysis it bears noting that it's eminently possible (if, it seems, not all that probable) for resources of both historicism and modernism to be productively employed in convincing architecture, so all is not necessarily lost (Fig. 3.23).

3.20
An object-building which, in its cartoonish parody of Collegiate Gothic (though unmeant as such) exemplifies a wrong way to emulate or respect historicism.

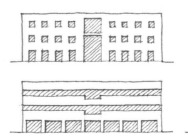

3.21
Modernist tropes in office buildings: window slots, punches, bands.

Institutions

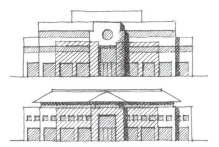

3.22
More modernist tropes in office buildings: corners, notches, overshirts, hipped roofscapes

3.23
Some pretty good somewhat historicist and somewhat modernist office buildings, each partaking to differing degrees of both historicism and modernism.

Office park buildings may come in rows or quads, may flank featureless ponds, and usually make only desultory efforts to hide their associated expanses of parking lot. True, larger campuses may feature parking garages which reduce the asphalt wide open spaces, but add their even-harder-to-dress-up building masses to the ensemble. On the inside, one or another suburban office park building may well continue to comprise a warren of individual offices and workrooms, despite west coastal startups having extolled the benefits of staffers roaming a wide-open interior with laptops in tow and perching wherever they care to amidst the "bleacher" lounge seating and foosball games. Indeed, the most egalitarian that a more typical corporate interior is likely to become will be to continue featuring the unloved cubicle, which at least provides a personal address and can accommodate small personal possessions, poignantly serving as reminders that one is not quite the cog in a machine that may often seem the case. It's true, though, that even this little corner of personal space is dwindling, with "U" shaped desktops becoming Ls – or Is –

3d.
Hospitals and Clinics

Hospitals are serious places, or more to the point, places where serious things are happening. Usually people are there because they are sick, or their loved ones are sick, or they are treating the sick. This being the case, hospitals should be anything *but* serious places as architecture, meaning their interiors should be rather colorful, light-filled, and easily understood. They should be designed to lift the spirit, at least a little bit – not so colorfully that it seems disingenuous or inappropriate – and to calm the anxious. These desirable attributes seem self-evident, and yet many hospital interiors seem to have had different goals in mind. Or perhaps no compelling perceptual goals at all, except for adjacencies: for managing to get the things next to or nearby each other that need it. Hospitals are so complex, and so ceaselessly under construction,

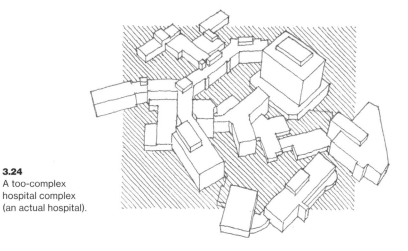

3.24
A too-complex hospital complex (an actual hospital).

3.25
A too-big hospital lobby.

that it can sometimes seem it is good enough if this one thing is sort of adequately achieved (Fig. 3.24). But the states of mind of hospital inmates are clearly affected by their surroundings, and their states of mind affect their states of health, or so it is written.

Arriving at the hospital is almost never a happy time. Well, maybe someone's having a baby: that could be one of very few exceptions. So, the non-happy arriver should be as unchallenged as possible by the initial experience. Has the reader never had a hospital arrival experience? Good for you, but you will, soon enough, and it will not be pleasant. Unfortunately, almost all hospitals have been added on to in a hodgepodge way over the years, often leading to a falling back onto directional graphics for orientation and direction: maybe there will be red lines this way, green lines that way, and so forth. Something else should be tried first, for while this may get someone headed in the right direction, it is a blunt-instrument sort of thing that does nothing to calm the arriver other than to send them, a cog in a machine, in a certain direction. "Wayfinding" being a whole specialized graphics discipline, argues it's best to leave the issue at that, except for the obvious enough caveat that there is good wayfinding design and there is not.

Big hospitals have a big tendency to have big lobbies: nothing like a Grand Central Station sort of ambiance to make someone feel lost and insignificant as well as non-happy on arrival (Fig. 3.25). How about an immediately understandable, not very high-ceilinged, cheerful enough space, with windows onto something other than the drop-off, and a living person not too far in the distance and not behind a window like it's the DMV, to tell you what to do? No visible electronic machines should be involved in this initial experience, though such a goal may now be all but impossible to achieve.

Again, hospitals are so complicated that every little common-sense thing that can be done to make getting around in them easier both for visitors and inmates should be done. One of these would be a general rule of adhering to right angles in space planning terms. A fad for triangular-plan patient floor modules took hold for a while: this should be resisted; orthogonal patient floors have worked fine for a hundred years and still do for most purposes, once the fine points of modern nursing practice have been taken into account. A new wing might appear to fit better if jammed in at an angle; this should be resisted as well, as should, at all costs, a faddish inclination to introduce angles in the plan just because it seems a cool thing to do. Planners have been known to do things like that for no better reason. A corridor may seem very long in a floor plan, but it's better to look down a long hallway than to come to a dogleg and wonder what to do next. A hallway experience can be broken up with various proportion, finish, or lighting changes, or better yet with windows partway down, or at the ends. And speaking of windows, it goes without saying that every room that can have one should – and if they cannot, why not – and that they should, of all things, be operable.

And never use those "cool white" fluorescents behind prismatic lenses; they make everyone look dead already and should have been replaced by LEDs long ago anyway.[3] But when taking down the troffers, don't take down the lay-in ceiling altogether. Bespoke buildings are going around topless nowadays with their entrails exposed overhead for all to see, as if anyone wanted to see all the mechanical and structural guts. Don't do it: hospitals probably want a washable ceiling in most places anyway, and it gives an unfortunate impression that the ceiling fell down in the night or something.

Clinics

Freestanding medical clinic buildings are similar to hospitals only in that sick people go to them also. But the same thing about being cheerful, though not too much, also applies. Clinics come in all sorts and sizes: primary care, physiotherapy, orthopedics, ophthalmology, cardiology, urology, dermatology, neurology, gastroenterology, gynecology, oncology, podiatry, ENT, pediatrics, geriatrics, dentistry, palmistry, addiction, nutrition, mental health — when you think about it the number of types is mind-boggling, and all of these are to be found in any self-respecting, medium-sized city. Plus, there are clinic adjacent places dealing in intravenous matters (plasma centers, dialysis clinics, infusion centers). It seems we're all sick with something or other most of the time. (Palmistry was there to see if you were paying attention, though those are clinics of sorts and at least as helpful as such pseudo clinics as supplement hucksters, homeopaths, or aromatherapy pyramid schemers.)

The following also applies also to hospitals: the dilemma of the waiting room chairs. Nobody wants to sit in long rows like at the airport. (And why is it that this is the way it is at the airport?) The less relentlessly space-efficient alternative, of arranging the chairs in little seating groups, comes with its own possible drawback of having to sit across from a probably unwell stranger for an indefinite and probably too long period. Ultimately versions of both kinds are probably needed and the answer, not too satisfactory but better than either, is to have both. And make them different seating kinds. In different colors. And some at angles, which, as opposed to the floor planning, can be a good idea. And make the appointment counter non-DMV-like while we're at it.

Natural light, or at least natural-like-light, is an important factor in the quality of a patient experience--or anyone's experience, for that matter. If the examining room, that tiny cubicle where you can almost hear what's going on in the next one, must have no windows at all, some sort of up light that will afford general even lighting is better than nothing (or the prismatic lens thing). If there aren't any windows in the examining rooms, at least have windows, or skylights, or something, in the area immediately outside the exam rooms. Clinics, like hospitals, tend to have big, squarish footprints and, as a result, much of the space is on the inner inside. But many clinics are on one level, so there's really no excuse in those cases for not having some sort of skylights or clerestories to ameliorate the sensation of having entered a cave, never to return. That sort of sensation is something you want to avoid in clinics and in hospitals.

Funeral Homes

No, it doesn't seem right for these to appear alongside hospitals and clinics, but there's a certain grim appropriateness to finding them here. They are the ultimate architectural resource for seeking to deal with the body's maladies, being death in this case. They have a way of looking a little like churches, or like mansions, or even branch banks of the traditional persuasion. Architecturally, there isn't really very much of a precedent to go by, the effort ending up being one of trying to appear accessible, friendly, dignified, and solemn all at the same time. They're more a service (a "stand-alone purveyor") than anything remotely like a clinic, though the carefully hidden back-of-house does deal in some rudimentary white-coat activities. Perhaps they're a sort of odd combo of a beauty parlor for the departed with a banquet or reception hall facility, focused on the same silent guest of honor. Years ago, there was a bit of deserved hue and cry about the sorry taking-advantage of the bereaved that was to be found in the industry. Thankfully the practice of burying some pickled remains in a $5,000 to $10,000 box is now less popular than cremation (itself still a bit sustainably suspect) and other less expensive, "greener" options.

---

3   LEDs come with their own pitfalls. Among the various color temperatures available among a confusing and inconsistent variety is something called "daylight," which is promoted as good for offices and kitchens. It may be heresy to say so but the author doesn't really think "daylight" has any place inside, excepting the real thing. It's said to be about the color temperature of a sunny day, but it's important to remember that a sunny day is about 10,000 footcandles while a normally bright interior is something like 30 or 40. At that level brilliant sunlight is transformed to a grimly drab and cold sort of illumination, even cooler than the already too cool cool-white. Further to the point, light shining directly down from overhead should be avoided generally, as it casts the eyes into shadow and thereby makes one look cadaverous, not a good look in a hospital.

private life the i bu

There's questionable design to be found in houses and apartments of all types and sizes, but the all-too-easiest to call out is the so-called "McMansion." These are the standouts among the pretty bad lot that has spread on out and caused the great American suburban sprawl.

rbs

004

4.1
Some period styles of the '20s.
Above: Colonial Revival,
Spanish Revival, Craftsman.
Below: Italian (or Mediterranean),
Dutch Colonial, Tudor.

4a.
McMansions: The Settings

Most would agree that the centerpiece of this taxonomy of everyday architecture would be the suburban house. It feels a little shameful to be writing critically about these because it's a bit like shooting fish in a barrel, really: there are so many things wrong, and so many of them that are painfully obvious. But apparently these aren't that obvious to builders or buyers. Well, that's an elitist statement, to be sure, but one is led more or less unavoidably to that conclusion. True, maybe buyers have little choice and make the best of a bad deal when it comes to the suburbs-- one has to give them that. Suburban residential development – sprawl – arose from a complex combo of land value, population growth, desire for more space, desire for better amenities, the car's ascendance – a bunch of issues. The deed is done, the burbs are here, and our mission now is simply to call out the bad to worse aspects that are ubiquitous in every city and town, in every state in the union, of millions of unaccountably bad houses.

The Type

A Field Guide to American Houses, by Virginia Savage McAlester, has been a remarkably useful and comprehensive classic since its first edition in 1984, with Lee McAlester. Its 2015 edition features significantly expanded coverage of metastatic variants on the American single-family house from the '90s to the present, and one defers to that edition for its efforts to taxonomize American house types and subtypes of that period. The emphasis here, with some digressions, will be on the particular "style" known therein as "Millennium Mansion," or elsewhere by the more widespread sobriquet "McMansion." An internet resource defines the latter as "a large modern house that is considered ostentatious and lacking in architectural integrity," a sentence elegant in the simplicity with which it sums up the two overarching negative attributes of millions of American homes.[1]

The above reference to a taxonomy suggests that the conundrum of the recent American house is a more complex animal than this one type. But the McMansion is its most visible and, indeed, its most readily critiqued manifestation. One surely hopes the view that its reign is in decline is correct, but despite such a development, the damage done remains extant and its impact widespread and long lasting.

Origins

To set the stage, one recalls the heritage of styles from Europe, including Tudor, Mediterranean, French, and neoclassical variants, that joined Colonial Revival and craftsman styles from new world precedents in the form of the period revivals that populated the suburbs of the '20s (Fig. 4.1). While these styles weren't perfect, they were pretty good, achieving attractive, varied, well-proportioned, and

---

1 A website titled "McMansion Hell," if still online, is worth checking out for some sharp commentary as well as some appalling images of the type.

Private Life in the Burbs

4.2
A Cape Cod house in Levittown, NY.

comfortable approaches to modest single family residential design, equipped with dependable sets of well-honed design specifics. But by the '30s, Europe had also spawned the advent of modernism in architecture, and this, along with the Great Depression and the impact of World War II, changed everything. The depression brought an end to the heyday of the period styles, and the war led in turn to mass housing estates of small, simple houses, often in the austere Cape Cod mold (Fig. 4.2). At the same time, the architectural profession was newly in thrall to the so-called International Style, arising most famously from the work and influence of Le Corbusier, Walter Gropius, Ludwig Mies van der Rohe, and their acolytes. So, demand for the period revivals — embodying convincing and deft designs drawn from informed knowledge of historical precedent — died out to no fault of their own, new house construction was simplified for economy and minimally embellished, and the profession left it all behind in any case for this new mistress. By the '50s, residential architecture in America had sort of lost its way.

Since the '30s the streetcar suburb had been replaced with the automobile suburb, and it was no longer necessary to walk to work or to the streetcar because we now had the privilege of getting out the car and driving to every single thing we needed or wanted to do. And as the '40s became the '50s and '60s, consumers wanted a step up from wartime austerity, and in large part the effect on the little Levittown Cape Cod was to stretch it laterally, with the "rancher" and its variants eventually cropping up throughout much of the nation (Fig. 4.3). It's true that some architects did some fine work in their preferred hothouse version of modernism (witness California's "Case Study Houses" as one set of examples),but architects were increasingly regarded as a luxury, hired by the privileged rather than the masses. Developers did make some inroads into mass market versions of what became known eventually as mid-century modern, Eichler Homes being one example, but their innovations were in the minority.

4.3
A rancher. Subtle adjustments — breaks in the roof or wall plane, extended window proportions — offered improvements to their relative dreariness.

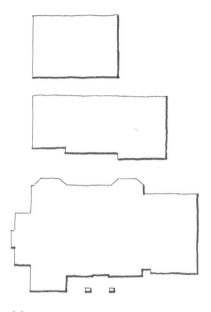

4.4
Comparative plan footprints:
Cape Cod, Rancher, McMansion.

By the '80s, the rancher itself, along with its clumsy variant, the split level,[2] had come to seem a bit inadequate to many members of the upwardly mobile middle class who wanted to step up yet again. Dazzled by well-publicized homes of the rich and grand, they wanted some of that grandeur for themselves. Toward this end, though, the quality equation clearly tilted in favor of quantity in the form of quickly built developments. The low profile of the rancher was finally and fully subsumed by two stories and a roof-of-roofs, and the footprint, already as wide as the lot and its setbacks allowed, was stretched in depth as well (Fig. 4.4). The result was a veritable cuboid of complex mansion-ish mass.

The roof would indeed become a complicated amalgamation of roofs, and in like manner the walls were developed with niches and notches and bays and recesses. Apparently, it came to be vaguely felt that a simple façade was somehow inappropriate, or maybe it was more to the point that a simple façade was hard to get right: somehow getting the proportions and disposition of the windows and doors just right was hard to achieve. The fact is that those skills were gone: the architects who knew them well in the '20s were long gone and those who'd come since not only didn't know them but didn't care to, being brave new modernists. It was the builders and developers who took up the challenge of giving the prospective owners what they thought they wanted and they had no more background in architectural history that either the modernist architects or the buyers of their McMansions.

To be sure, that knowledge would have been directly available in the public library (though not online, for it's sometimes hard to remember that Google and Wikipedia didn't exist in the '80s and '90s). In any case, it seems as if the developers preferred to follow the lead of what the last guy did in the pursuit of what sold well, or what they saw in trade journals, or whatever, along with a sort of a felt compulsion to be original. Or at the least, a tendency to make things up from scratch without reference to some background knowledge on whether they might necessarily work aesthetically. It's even possible that this compulsion found some of its roots in the modernism that the McMansion builders avoided, for the origins of modernism arose from a turning aside from the "old, tired styles of the past." The fact that modernism in its assorted flavors has itself demonstrated an adherence to trends rather than originality in design is, of course, an irony of note in passing. Another irony with respect to 20th century residential architecture is the fact that, in its pursuit of modernism, the

---

2 The split level was arguably useful if the property sloped from side to side, although often enough this was not even the case. In short, it was bit of a gimmick, often requiring a half flight of exterior steps to reach the front door and then further half-flights to reach the fully upstairs and the fully downstairs. The so-called bi-level was worse, trading an on-grade front door for half-flights within from the foyer to everything else. True, its lower level sometimes opened to grade at the back making this a front-to-back split level, sort of. The split level tended to look a bit like evidence of a geological fault in its past, while the bi-level's front door aligned with nothing else on the front elevation.

architectural profession lost most of the work to be had in single family residential design in America by mid-century. The builders were in charge, and maybe they had an architecture graduate in the back room or maybe they didn't, for in fact, by and large, the stamp of a registered architect was not required to build their houses.

The "originality" demonstrated by the work of the McMansion designers did arise in part from an accumulation of those hazy recollections of historicist pieces and parts, but lacking reference to actual precedents, the relationships among the parts—to say nothing of the parts themselves—were not handled well. Back in the '20s, not only were builders cognizant of (or at least surrounded by) convincingly realized revival styles, they also had the benefit of low-paid, old-world craftsmen to build and enhance them. By the second half of the last century, craftsmen were no longer willing to work for low wages, and they no longer knew anything much about revival styles, if indeed true craftsmen of any sort could be found. An analogy can perhaps be found in the world of journalism, which in the 21st century has become seriously compromised by the world of "social media"; in short, a sea change, due to the utter convenience of the internet, from writing by professionals about facts and opinions to writing by amateurs about opinions only. The analogy, sort of, sees architects as design professionals having been supplanted by builders as design amateurs. To be sure, there's no pesky architect's fee, but it holds true here that you get what you pay for. And it bears noting that, in some cases, the owners themselves—no more experienced in design than were the builders—helmed the design of their own McHomes.

The builders had a bit more to go on than hazy recollections, though, for a particular influence in those times came from the architects' architecture of the period, newly under the thrall of something called postmodernism. Modernism having finally become boring, at least to some, this style involved the "witty" distortion or excerpting of classical elements and motifs in bespoke and not-so-bespoke architecture of the times. Often enough, these efforts made a bit too much fun of their precedents, and the McMansion builders who noticed this happening were prone to taking that license to heart, with some unfortunate and ill-informed results.

The Neighborhood

As mentioned in the earlier discussion of shopping centers, many years ago when in grade school in Kansas City, the author was occasionally sent on foot to the corner grocery about three blocks from home for a few provisions. He also walked, unwillingly, to said grade school, about five blocks away. (The E. F. Swinney School is now senior apartments. The grocery building's also still there, a charming little Tudor/French Provincial agglomeration with a cone-hatted corner tower fronting a little intersection, although it looks to be more about upscale accessories, flowers, chocolate, and coffee nowadays.) (Fig. 1.3). The point of this nostalgic sidebar: walkability of that sort is long gone for much of the world of suburban residential development that has come along since.

To be more accurate, in terms of the 'burbs it was never there. Schools have become those big boxy things miles away featuring long lines of SUVs dropping off and picking up offspring despite the existence of school bus routes. And the corner store seems generally not to exist, even though its merits seem obvious. Zoning does have a way of prohibiting such things, and the mindset of suburban neighborhoods does them no favors either, fears of "an element" hanging out there, perhaps. Ultimately though it comes down to economics: with sprawl-houses on lots of a quarter-acre or more there's just no viability in a walkable corner store. Instead, we have the ubiquitous strip center, well known for its signal lack of architectural merits and its utter lack of walkability for most suburbanites.

Of course, corner stores and other neighborhood amenities do exist. Some older grid-type residential blocks in older cities feature small markets which, while lacking an economic benefit of scale, do at least tend to have desirable societal benefits. Corner bars are also to be found there, amenities having their own pros and cons. A selection of "new urbanist" developments also features such amenities, and they are walkable, sometimes. But in the big picture, the dead-end-roaded suburbs are the rule, each development separated from the next despite the cul-de-sac of one mere yard from those of the next, all flowing like little brooks to the fast-flowing streams of connector roads leading to more of the same (Fig. 4.5).

4.5
The suburban non-grid.

The Site

The McMansion site may be a quarter acre, a half-acre, or even an acre or more, a range that seems typical for sprawl subdivisions from mid-last-century to the present day.[3] Inevitably — virtually without exception — there is a front lawn, laboriously maintained, often by a team of the less privileged that comes in a truck with a trailer. Their equipment can generally be heard all day long in the spring. In the fall, gas-powered leaf blowers can also be heard, and among those with the questionable judgment to live in the north, gas-powered snow blowers can be heard in the winter. Leaving us with the summer, when the grass, of course, still needs to be mowed, again resulting in loud equipment, dawn to dusk.

Xeriscaping is an excellent alternative to the maintenance that a flat living surface requires. Consisting of native plant materials along with mulch, gravel, stone, or other non-turf ground cover, this has been quite successful in the southwest. But the turfgrass of the non-southwest is a different story, wherein pollinators find no habitat, birds may ingest seeds infused with pesticides, and rainwater runoff carries fertilizers to downstream watercourses. A variety of strategies for "no-mow" yards do exist, being good environmentally, aesthetically, and upkeep-wise, but these are

---

3   While the bulk of this critique does concern a scale of that sort, it bears noting that a corresponding scale of about an eighth an acre is also ubiquitous, and just as subject to the concerns laid out here. Or perhaps not as much, really, as there is simply less in the way of physical opportunity to err. Not to say that there haven't been many attempts to insert McMansions on too-small lots. (See "Smaller Houses in the Burbs.")

rarely seen. It's too bad that it seems difficult to break the cycle of keeping up with the neighbors when it comes to turf matters.

Side Yards and Back Yards

Depending on the relative width of the property and of the house, side yards are minimally useful to not useful at all, though normally requiring the same turf maintenance as the front yard. But a palazzo, villa, mansion, chateau, manor – these being the prototypes of the estates that suburban houses seem to aspire to, image wise – require as much surrounding space as possible to further their dominant status. Hence the useless side yards. Again, it's about keeping up appearances or, more to the point, dominating in appearance terms, if possible, though it's pretty difficult for every property to dominate--impossible, really.

The front porch as a place to spend time, sipping lemonade and observing passersby, is a fondly conjured fantasy of long-ago domestic life, a situation that was the norm around the turn of the last century, having never existed during the lives of present-day suburban denizens. In any case, we don't really care to allow others to see what we're doing while at home, other than a certain amount of earnest effort wrestling the plant materials around the front lawn. Simply sitting on the front porch, assuming it is even deep enough to comfortably accommodate porch furniture, which it often is not, would be unbecoming even in the largest of suburban "estates." Evidence of an excess of spare time on the part of the porch sitters would seem unseemly, the American way being a public display of energy and initiative, possibly regarding that maintenance of the ornamental plantings. Of course, as noted, the maintenance of the lawn itself, not to mention the exterior features and roofs of the house, is generally done by proletarian helpers in the sorts of suburban contexts that are our subject.

The suburban backyard is where it's at. At least symbolically sheltered from the always curious view of others, it's where familial at-home outdoor activities transpire. And while no expense is spared on maintaining the front yard, it is here where truly lavish expenditures are often made. Depending on the income and relative profligacy of the owner, these may include massive grilles, outdoor kitchens, spas, terraces, porches that have their own porches, and, of course, swimming pools. Until recently, these were the ultimate display of conspicuous consumption, consuming water in vast amounts and requiring mechanical maintenance, cleaning, covering, uncovering, and security fencing, which will have been wisely required by code to prevent the inadvertent drowning of neighborhood pets or children. The ever correct internet tells us that a swimming pool may increase the value of one's house by up to 7%, but that the cost to install the pool may exceed this number. And that a house may well be more difficult to sell if it features a pool.

The author remembers his grandparents' little postwar house in Waukesha, Wisconsin, one of those basic Cape Cods, with a duly maintained little lawn in front and a lovely *tapis vert* in back surrounded by foundation plantings, paving stones, a complete little vegetable and flower garden, a tiny shed, and a one-car garage facing an alley. This rear yard ensemble truly seemed an outdoor room, so well-defined by the house, garage, garden, and modest fences on the sides. And the alley was the ideal organizer for the block, serving the garages and trash cans while also being a presentable-enough entry route. But alleys aren't a part of the subdivision plan in most of the more recent suburbs in question, and it's a good question why not. For one thing, without them we often have the challenge of how to deal with facing the back neighbor's back yard, two private outdoor realms thus affording not-so-private views of each other. One wonders, though, whether it isn't simply a matter of economics: no alley means one less road to have paid for providing and maintaining. Neighborhood dwellers thus have the privilege of hauling out the trash toters to the front curb on pickup days, and of welcoming the lawn people or package delivery people or maintenance people at the same curb, their vehicles encumbering the street while they're there.

Back at the front curb, we approach the McHouse itself, the too-big elephant in the room.

4c.
McMansions: The Outsides

The pieces and parts that make up the exteriors of McMansions are the same basic elements that make up a wide spectrum of residential architecture: it's the ways in which they are used or misused that render them grist for the mill of this critique. Such misusage can range from simply having too many elements crowded onto the McMansion exterior, or having them arranged in ill-proportioned ways, sometimes to appalling extremes of design and construction ineptitude.

Windows, present in most buildings in one form or another, afford a surprising array of ways to get it wrong. The Palladian window or "serliana" is one, featuring an arched central opening flanked by flat-headed windows. A baffling yet common enough McMansion error pulls the spring of the arch inboard from the dividing pilasters or columns, such that the very points that require support are left hanging in midair (Fig. 4.6). Round arches such as the serliana's usually feature keystones, signifying stability of the arch, but often enough the keystone is omitted, resulting in a sort of irresolute, unstable quality. Also often missing from arch-topped windows are horizontal members at the spring line of the arch, contributing further to visual instability.

It's no bad thing to vary the elements on a large façade, which McMansions usually have, but as with most things it's all a matter of degree, and often the elements are both too varied and too numerous. A good rule of thumb with windows is to keep the number of different types to a minimum, or at least to employ a number of types that fall within a family of a particular sort. This is often not the case, though, and we have assortments of big ones, small ones, tall ones, square ones, and windows with round tops, segmentally arched tops, or even the unfortunate innovation of quarter-circular tops. In a brick-clad façade, windows may sadly feature a stone-ish surround like a picture frame, without regard for the differing natures of head, jamb, and sill. Or there may be no surround at all, with a soldier course at best spanning across the head, expressive of the window as little more than a hole cut out of brick-design wallpaper.

Shutters are whole other subject. Some designers like to make fun of shutters because, to be sure, it's been centuries since shutters actually served to shut. (Well, maybe they still do on occasion in hurricane country.) But this fact is immaterial: the main function served by shutters has long been one of abstract compositional enhancement. Absent a highly textured or variegated cladding material, window openings that are spaced apart to serve a variety of interiors have a way of looking a bit lonesome or isolated. (It bears restating that we are dealing in the context of revival style façades rather than modernist ones, the latter being a subject for an entirely different narrative.) In short, shutters broaden the statement made by a window while also variegating it. They even provide an opportunity for adding color, though that can also be an opportunity for disaster in the wrong hands. Color aside, there are only a couple of other matters to get right when it comes to shutters: that they should, taken together, be the same width as the window, or at least a decent effort made in that direction, and, if they are attached to the wall rather than the jamb, that this shameful fact should at least not be too apparent. Finally, regarding shutters on round topped windows, the best course would be to not include the round top in the shuttering at all. But if this is unavoidable for some baffling reason, the quarter round curve of each shutter top should mirror the round top, not the other way around—which has happened! All that said, it's well to keep one's eyes open for situations that don't necessarily call for shutters, because, for one thing, they're suitable mainly for Colonial Revival or neoclassical designs and less so otherwise. Not that this has stopped their proliferation among what, once called the revival styles, have become the mishmash thereof.

Wood siding may occasionally make its appearance among the McMansions, but the predominant cladding material is brick veneer. Or at least in front. The sides and rear may be where wood or wood-like siding appears instead, since an occasional cost-saving dodge is to limit the more expensive material to the front, the sides being, of course, invisible. (And

   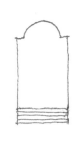

4.6
A Serliana (left) and assorted incorrect variants.

indeed, they may more-or-less be, given the narrow dimensions of side yards.) But the practice inevitably imparts a cheap, cut-and-glued quality (Fig. 4.7). Given a perspective of history, the practice is in fact revealed as doubly or triply cheap, brick having originally been the actual solid wall material, with stone – or stucco, itself stone's cheaper substitute – having been the veneer. Anyway, brick has the advantage and capability of varied color and texture, though this can also be a problem as both variables can be and frequently are misused. For one example, when a "full range" of brick color is specified, it will fall to the masons to make sure the lighter or darker bricks are evenly intermixed with the basic color (darker brick having been on the outsides of the batch in the kiln). This seldom happens. (It bears noting that this is an issue with every building where brick is used and not just with the McMansions.)

Stone, in turn, can appear in the form of synthetic veneer products designed to be laid in a variety of ashlar type patterns, and one must grudgingly admit that these can sometimes be fairly convincing. Well enough is not left alone, however, for stone will occasionally be laid up *on edge*, an approach characterized by a wild assortment of angles and shapes on the wall having the sole benefit of economy (Fig. 4.8). It appears either as flattish veneer or as actual massive stonework called "uncoursed random rubble." But flat stone veneer laid on edge *can* look good in a mid-century modern application if the stone is very flat and the joints are very narrow. And, famed architect Le Corbusier featured convincing versions of this approach on a number of his projects. So clearly the matter, like so many such subjective matters, is complicated.

Speaking of stucco, this honorable finish is not very widely used in modern times, its place having been taken by EIFS (Exterior Insulation and Finish System), or more colloquially, Dryvit, that having been the trade name of the initial such product on the market. This assembly of materials exists for the purpose of providing builders and developers with something cheaper than brick or decent siding but not quite as cheap as vinyl, aluminum, or texture 1-11.[4] Aside from being less prone to cracking than stucco and affording a sort of minimal insulation benefit, it has few other merits. It affords someone with a boxcutter a simple and direct way to break into a building that is clad therewith, being foamboard coated with plastic mesh and a sort of cement-based paint. It provides McMansions that are lined up in rows with a way to vary their façades, specifically to downgrade the look of the houses so clad. EIFS simply does not look the same as cement plaster (stucco), for its inherent cheapness seems to shine through, due in part to wobbly edges, irresolute corners, and erratic surfaces that are neither smooth nor roughcast. Another problem, masquerading as

4.7
Brick on the front only. (More likely to be seen on houses with actual budgets than on fully fledged McMansions. (See "Smaller Houses in the Burbs.")

4.8
Stone veneer laid on edge, usually resulting in a clumsy, crazy-quilt look.

---

4 "Decent siding" refers either to solid wood siding, or the better versions of composition siding (made of cement, sand, and cellulose fibers), colloquially known as Hardie Board for a well-known supplier of the product. It does not refer to aluminum siding or vinyl siding. Vinyl siding, seen more often on apartment or starter home developments, has the advantage of being cheaper than anything else, and the disadvantages of tending to fade, crack and buckle, of displaying its thinness in unsightly visible seams and wavy edges, and of ultimately sitting in landfills for eternity. "Texture 1-11," another colloquial term arising from a trade name, means plywood that has been channeled vertically at 8" intervals, serving thereby to fail at simulating tongue-and-groove wood siding while also exposing the outer plies to weathering at 8" intervals. The 4' x 8' product also reveals its surpassingly cheap nastiness by adopting a slightly wavy profile if not carefully installed, which it will not be.

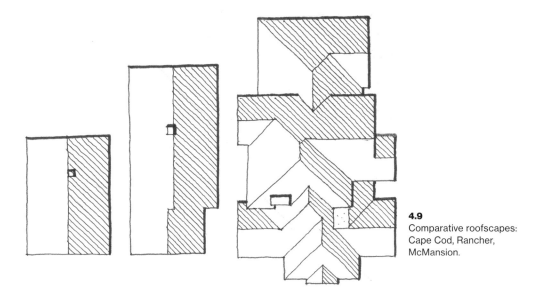

4.9
Comparative roofscapes: Cape Cod, Rancher, McMansion.

an advantage, is that foamboard can be and is cut to shape as sills, headers, quoins, and cornices. Indeed, all such shapes and more are available precut from manufacturers, enabling the entire decorated façade to be made of a material that attracts dirt, has had notorious problems with moisture, could blow away in the wind if it wasn't glued down, and kind of looks that way as well. To give them their due, Dryvit and its ilk have tried diligently to fix some of those problems, though the appearance issues, well...

The Roof

Or one should say the roofs. The ranch, the split level, the contemporary—indeed most all the variants of the single-family house until the '80s or so—had simple roofs, a gable, a hipped gable, or a shed if daringly raffish, often with a simple cross gable for variety. But with the hypertrophied houses to come, a need was somehow felt for elaborated roofs in keeping with their more massive scale. With hips on hips, gables on gables, and/or gables on hips, these newly complex roofs were and are chock full of ridges and valleys, each an invitation for trouble or, at the very least, finicky construction (Fig. 4.9). Dormers, chimneys, and cupolas added their own flashing and shingling complexities. Speaking of shingles, wood or wood-like shakes and slate or slate-like shingles made their appearances on occasion, but the predominant roof shingle was asphalt. The reliable three-tab model came to be considered far too mundane—too flat and rancher-like—for the McOwner, so "dimensional" shingles came about, often looking rather like a whole series of mistakes had been made during the stapling-down and adhering process. But no, the shaggy and irregular look was deliberate, even though it really resembled neither shakes nor slates, and a too-wide variegation in lighter and darker tones took the irregular look further yet.

Shingling is just the beginning of complexity and cost for these roofs, the framing within having become a forest of dimensional lumber, rife with special lengths and special ends. In comparison, the rancher roof was simplicity itself, with gang nailed gable trusses that were lightweight and prefabricated, afforded a clear span, and were all but identical, end to end. True, the flat eight-foot ceilings within were low and unvaried, and one must agree that some variety was desirable.[5] But as so often happens, the presence of a happy medium between economy and variety was sped right past in the search for distinctive variegation in the roofscape, and the endless ridges and valleys required endless adjustments in the lengths and bearings of the now relatively heavy members, with none of the economies afforded by trusses.

---

5   One ingenious variant on the gable truss, affording some measure of that very variety, was the scissors truss, which still permitted a clear span while also providing a pitched ("vaulted") ceiling.

As one more recurring exterior element that links the roof to the ground via the wall, gutters and downspouts have a way of being very visible afterthoughts regardless of the house style. Barring the use of gutters incorporated into the cornice or downspouts incorporated in the wall, which are nearly unheard of in residential architecture of this ilk, these necessities end up being surprisingly prominent features, sparring with more intentionally decorative elements for attention — and they tend to be *absent* from developers' renderings. It doesn't help that standard profiles are a fussy ogee (S-like) shape for the gutter and an unsightly ribbed box for the downspout. Semicircular gutters supported on brackets and unribbed round downspouts would be preferred, yet, sadly, more expensive. And it's wrong to have called them necessities; gutters, so prone to filling with up leaves and giving us entertaining newspaper ads for gutter screen devices — or downspouts, with their corresponding need for unsightly splash blocks or peculiar extensions — may be *omitted* in some cases if the grades below that thereby receive rainwater can be properly treated and graded.

The Garage

Back in the '20s, the garage, if there was one, held one car and was usually located behind the house, either with a driveway to the street in front or, more directly, to an alley in back. The interior of the garage left just enough space around the edge to drive nails into the 2x4s and sheathing boards for hanging up your rakes and shovels. Nowadays, of course, the garage is marketed as a missed opportunity to provide a self-respecting great-room ambiance for your cars. In thus taking our first peek in a McMansion interior, we may find an epoxy floor, painted gypboard walls and ceiling, base and wall cabinets, and perhaps a fireplace or a wet bar, who knows. It's cars plural of course, now more likely meaning three, a two-car garage being so '80s. That said, even the two-car garage, typically facing the same direction as the front door, offered something of a challenge to builders by sometimes being half the width of the façade.

The *three*-car garage was and is necessarily divided into single and double doors, one of them often projected a bit with its own subsidiary gable as an unconvincing "breaking up the scale" gesture. To be sure, the garage sometimes faced the side, or the back, or was a wing to the front with the driveway cutting across the rest of the façade, thus partially dealing with that pesky problem of what to do with the front yard. In such cases, the blank garage side wall now facing the road will have been embellished with a large window offering generous daylight for the car's indoor activities, and perhaps a subsidiary gable or bay here as well. Why three garage spaces? Well, the 16-foot-long SUV (or perhaps a 19-foot-long super cab pickup) was apparently an essential, though for reasons that are difficult to determine in the absence of daily soccer team duties or a side hustle in the moving or contracting business. A second car for a spouse is also required, in all probability being another SUV, and perhaps a sporty number is needed as well for occasions when a small bus just seems inappropriate. Odds are that a teenage or fully-grown scion also resides there and needs secure, climate-controlled parking to boot. All things considered, a three-car garage may seem barely adequate. It goes without saying that the garage is incorporated into the volume of the house since it is, after all, almost always the owners' entranceway, so we can forget the merits of a detached garage off an alley. Finally, should there be any further vehicles or vehicle-like objects belonging to the household that don't have spaces in the garage, and there will be (these may include motorboats, ORVs, or golfcarts for the elementary and junior high crowd to joyride about in, etc.), they will be decoratively ganged on the driveway, or on a driveway extension which helpfully further reduces the size of front lawn, or in the road itself along with the lawn guy's.

The Entrance

The house types that preceded the McMansion and its variants typically had understated entries. The houses of Frank Lloyd Wright are said to have influenced the design of the rancher, with its long, low lines, and the same could be said of the front door, which he almost invariably tucked in a recess and under a low soffit. But evidently this had come to be seen as too self-effacing somehow: the upwardly mobile of the McMansion's heyday were proud of their ability and willingness to max out their credit cards and seem to have felt that the entrance should, correspondingly, be a proud and prominent feature. There may have been some hazy recollection of the elaborated pediments

4.10
Some McM front façades (grande arch and bitsy porch versions), with their multifarious windows, gables, bays, and roofs. While sometimes not so bad in individual terms, these elements get combined in unbalanced and overdone varieties.

of Georgian houses or of some grand neoclassical entry porches – those made a special occasion of the front door, did they not? So, McMansion entries tended to be one and a half or two-story affairs, topped by a round arch, framing a shallow recess of corresponding height at the front door, itself surmounted with some version of especially dramatic window, the whole serving no function of shelter, and its proportions appearing stretched out of shape vertically, which indeed they were (Fig. 4.10). While a variety of other attention-seeking entry ensemble configurations were tried, this was the favorite. The house's broad and hodge-podge ensemble of pieces and parts needed a focus, and the entrance was seized upon in some measure of desperation to provide it. None of these comments gainsay the fact that the owners entered via the garage, and that the front entrance was there only for visitors and, most importantly, as a badge of domestic achievement.

Sometimes the front door was ensconced in a front porch, which was no longer a place to tempt anyone to tarry in the shade with a cardboard fan from the funeral home in hand, but merely another way to enhance the grandeur of arrival. Aside from its roof, pediment, or surmounting balcony, the defining elements of a porch are its columns, and their incorrect deployment is the rule rather than the exception when porches are added to the McMansion mix. The particular issues involved in their deployment are spacing (intercolumniation), proportion, and detail, and in truth there are a lot of exceptions proving the rules when it comes to these matters, making it easier than ever to not get them very right. Column spacing, for example, must be equal, except for when there is a good reason for it to not be, one example being a colonnade made up of paired columns instead of single ones. And columns may in fact be quite thin, as long as they are in proportion to the roof or pediment above and the doors or windows beyond, which they often are not. And if they are round rather than square, columns should have entasis – that subtle swelling and shrinking of the profile – lest they appear as graceful as the cardboard tube remaining from the paper towels. Some correct version of base, capital, and roof beam or pediment or entablature or something, as opposed to nothing, would also be helpful, as these pieces and parts are sometimes inadequate to the purpose, or simply omitted. Thus, we stand here on the threshold, about to enter and see if the McMansion insides measure up in error-prone grandeur to the outsides.

Private Life in the Burbs

4d.
McMansions: The Insides

Ranchers, with their unvarying eight-foot ceilings, seem to have prompted McMansion designers to think bigger, taller, or both. But the problem as always was a matter of degree, interior spaces often ending up being both too big *and* too tall. Our too tall archway outside the front door leads directly to the too tall entrance hall. A favorite device here is a bridge overhead, connecting two sides of the second floor and marking a transition to the equally too tall "great room" beyond. But there's hardly a transition, really, since both spaces compete equally in their overscale grandiosity. One or the other should be lower for a satisfactory sequence to exist. In that regard, if the entrance hall is grand and tall, it would fall to the living area to be low and sheltering, but this sequence risks seeming an anticlimax. On the other hand, were the entrance area low and intimate (as Frank Lloyd did so well) and the living area tall and grand, the latter would risk seeming anything but inviting and intimate (and indeed, FLW never really understood living rooms, with his endless banquettes forcing guests to line up like birds on a wire). The point is that all this tallness and bigness has forgotten about the nature of modern-day domestic interiors. We no longer assemble lords and ladies in the hall of honor before being bade to enter the throne room, yet it seems that a desire for regal grandness has infused the McMansion interior, leaving only smaller peripheral spaces to afford inviting or intimate scale, which they may or may not since those tend to be afterthoughts. In short, the grand entrance hall serves no sequential function in the experience of the interior, but as a boastful gesture only, while the great room—the very name indicative of the overscale ambitions it is to embody—serves poorly as a space for domestic repose (Fig. 4.11).[6] Seating arrangements tend to be at sea, floating about without anchors, often dealing with through-passing circulation routes that break them up further.

---

6   But what, one may ask, of Spanish Revival numbers that sometimes feature tall living rooms? These are successful because their proportions haven't been allowed to grow excessively in all directions. And they typically feature axially oriented roof framing that lends a sense of order, while adjoining lower-ceilinged areas anchor and contrast with the tall space.

4.11
A "great room."

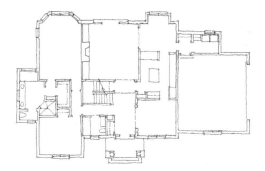

4.12
An McM floor plan. This layout, which does manage to avoid pointless angles and extended wings, is actually rather well-mannered and more reasonably assembled than many horrors out there. But not a single room is at all well-equipped with natural light, or cross-ventilation either. Note the kitchen buried in the middle, and the characteristic entry hall/bridge/great room sequence.

The Fireplace

There must be a primal hearth in the lord's manor, though a wood box may be unnecessary as the hearth may actually be a "gas log" or even just a row of little jets that pathetically symbolize the absent actual flames. While it situates best if opposite the main windows, that plan is unlikely, as the space will probably be leaking out into the entrance hall there. A fallback would be a side wall, where it and the inevitable flat screen above it compete to preside over the GR. But it's equally likely that the fireplace will have ended up on the *outside* wall, where it competes for attention with views to the back 40, the two opposed "prospect and refuge" experiences thereby conflated into one with the resulting diminishment of each.[7] (And it should be admitted that this very misstep is often made in custom designed houses of the minimalist modernist persuasion as well.)

A couple of further variations on the fireplace may reluctantly be mentioned. One is the two-sided version, especially popular in the '60s, which has the advantage of serving two rooms simultaneously (or, more realistically, there effectively being one combined room with a fireplace obstructing its central area), and the disadvantages of having thus compromised a working firebox by eliminating its back wall, and of having no sense of arrival or containment for the "fire experience." The other variant would be the shoved-in-the-corner fireplace, seeming a last-resort measure of an inept space planner, that cuts across at a diagonal and serves no known seating arrangement well.

The Kitchen

For quite a while the kitchen has presided as the apogee of the residential interior, situated as it usually is for ready access to the great room, dining room, breakfast nook, entrance hall, and garage. All this will have had a tendency to nudge the kitchen toward the physical center of the house, and since the house is now cuboidal, this will render the kitchen largely lacking in either natural light or cross ventilation. Though it's true that these attributes may well be considered hopelessly old fashioned in our modern encapsulated age. More generally, any space of any consequence that finds itself in the middle of the front, side, or back of the McM will also lack for much of either attribute, the GR being a prime example (Fig. 4.12). And for that matter, the corner rooms in this example are equally lacking and for no good reason. Finally, one can't help but notice that, in contrast to the rectangular simplicity of the basic rancher, this plan's perimeter sports fully 28 inside and outside corners.

But back to the lordly kitchen, where startlingly expensive and large-scale appliances, clad in oddly industrial-looking stainless steel and capable of feats the typical homeowner really has no need or ability for, compete for admiration. There are interior design specialists who deal with nothing but kitchens, hardly surprising given the endless opportunities for nook-and-crannyism the kitchen affords. Snooping in the slide-out shelves in the self-closing cupboards, we may find custom-crafted cubbies for each and every color-coordinated peeler, pizza cutter, and avocado tool. Homeowners who wish

---

7   These terms refer to a theory of the experience of landscape which holds that there are deep seated human predilections, arising from the experience of our genetic forebears, for places of prospect (wherein one can see over a great distance) and of refuge (a place where one can hide). Wright's residential architecture is thought to notably emulate these contrasting spatial experiences.

Private Life in the Burbs

to embody the lifestyles of the rich and famous, despite partaking of neither attribute, may wish for kitchen subsidiaries such as the walk-in pantry, butler's pantry, wet bar, or flower room; after all, it's only money.

The Other Living-ish Rooms

The great room standing revealed in the cold light of day (a pretty dim light in much of the GR) as a not particularly inviting space when it comes down to it, one should not gainsay the proud McMansion owners of alternatives that may serve more adequately for daytime interior functions. Any or all of parlors, libraries, studies, dens, and rec rooms may be found, the number of them corresponding to the degree of the owners' willingness to pay for, furnish, decorate, heat, cool, illuminate, and maintain them. As with the kitchen, though, the eyes may be bigger than the stomach, so to speak. Ultimately the role of such spaces in the McM would seem to be important, in that they're likely to be the locales where significant portions of domestic daytime are spent once the GR has proven to be sort of uninviting. But maybe we are missing something, and perhaps that cavern, that abyssal expanse, is just what was desired. Well, probably not, really, since the owners may simply not realize that they could be more comfortable in a more domestically scaled space. It does seem when it comes down to it that we can get used to most anything. Or perhaps the owners are away at work all the time making money to support their big house habit, their great rooms being used mainly for entertaining. Sadly, this may be truer that one would like to believe.

One mustn't forget the deluxe ancillaries to the living and living-ish rooms, which are, in reality, the privilege of the most very privileged. These would include the wine room, for example, or the home theater. A game room at the very least, or a billiard room, or a couple of bowling alleys.[8] These will adjoin the home bar. A home gym will be desirable, perhaps with dressing rooms situated so they can also serve the sauna or the indoor swimming pool. It would be nice to conclude that the sort of wealth that appreciates and can afford such ultimate niceties also appreciates good design in such enhancements, but sadly this is seldom, perhaps rarely, the case, for what frequently results instead is simply an even larger McM.

The Lesser Bedrooms

There's not a lot to be said about these, which tend to be on the small side, often sharing a bathroom of oddly normal dimensions off the hallway. Sometimes the bathroom will have doors directly from two bedrooms instead, thereby both compromising privacy and rendering the bath inaccessible from the hall. The bedroom doors may partake of an overly ingenious 45-degree angled orientation, such angles often cropping up in the floor plan generally as attempts to paper over errors in the jigsaw arrangement of rooms, corridors, and closets. A whole forthrightly angled wing is fine if confidently devised, but pointless little jigs and jogs add both construction expense and detract from a sense of interior resolution and repose, should that be something anyone cares about.

The Master Suite

It may be that, in addition to nighttime time, this is actually where some of that daytime time is spent: there's certainly enough room. Casting our eyes back for a moment to those '50s ranchers, they tended to be laid out on the interior in side-by-side halves: on one side, living room in front, dining ell and kitchen in back; on the other, three bedrooms and a bath. One bath! One bedroom slightly larger with a slightly larger closet with sliding doors. An attached garage, first for one car, soon enough for two. This nostalgic recall is not meant to promote such a plan as necessarily desirable in any way, but to cast a light upon the enormous degree to which our domestically interior expectations have changed. For one thing, the master bedroom (which it seems we shall now call the main or primary bedroom out of fears that the "master" term will be offensive in some unlikely way) is now as removed as possible from the lesser bedrooms. Nowadays, having put up with our offspring (or guests) in the daytime, it seems we want to be far away after hours, and the master suite (MS) is thereby provided with enough space to indeed serve as a satellite living room: a deluxe redoubt where one might stay indefinitely were it not for the lack of a kitchen (though master suites have actually been known to feature satellite kitchens).

---

8   Billiard rooms were common in upper-upper-middle class British houses in the before-TV days, as something to keep the men busy, along with brandy and cigars and all that, while the ladies withdrew to the (with)drawing room to talk over actual matters. Some gilded age manses even featured bowling or skittle alleys.

Just as the kitchen is the heart of the home, the master bath has somehow become the heart of the MS. It certainly rivals the bedroom itself in size, being truly a tiled salon of opulent magnificence. The twin vanities, the toilet nook, the walk-in shower, the freestanding tub in front of the picture window serving fantasies of reclining in amidst rose petals and candles, are arrayed with space-consuming grandeur. There may even be one of those two-sided fireplaces, shared with the bedroom. Oddly enough, more often than not, the walk-in closet is now entered from the bath, perhaps to reduce the bedroom's growing proliferation of doorways. "Closet" is, of course, a hopelessly inadequate term for a space that can be as big as a rancher's living room, wherein one's accoutrements of attire may repose in respectful dignity. There are closet specialists to help out with providing a cubby for each shoe and chapeau, these experts also being at one's disposal to consult on those garage enhancements. Chaise longues may render the room available for lounguing should the MS as well as the great room have become uninviting.

The Last Analysis

Having had that walk-through, we are left to ponder, what's really so wrong with all that? The upwardly mobile wannabees wanted it that way, and they got it, and they're happy, or happy enough. Why is it our business to complain, to be so bold as to criticize their taste, like the elitists we apparently are? Setting aside mere existential issues like the environmental disaster that are the suburbs of which we speak, it comes down to the reality that while these home dwellers may think they're happy, their lives could be more fulfilling and consequential if they knew more about the good and bad effects of different aspects of a living environment. It's a sad story of the perpetuation of ignorance on the part of the builders, the designers, and the would-be owners and dwellers. It's not their fault, really, or it's everyone's fault-- ultimately, society's-- one might boldly offer that public education, or the lack of it, is to blame for many of the shortcomings of everyday architecture.

So what, in the last analysis, is the thing about residential styles in the suburbs? It's probably best not to go all the way back to checking out their origins in antiquity, for the subject at hand is, after all, everyday architecture in America. But it bears

4.13
A New Traditional house, being Colonial Revival of a sort in this case. It's a big step up from an McM, though scale and balance issues remain problematic. New Traditional designs crop up in varied rediscoveries of the '20s revivals, usually being both bigger and less well-done; they have been somewhat better done in recent times.

4.14
A Seaside Cracker house.

noting that various and sundry revivals first had their reign in the USA in the 19th century, their forebears having dated as far back as the 1600s in the case of colonial originals. What were, thereby, actually re-revivals then came along in the early part of the 20th century, as noted in an earlier chapter. *Re-re-revivals* of a sort then emerged as mid-century approached, these being rather weak-willed pastiches of bits of period styles stuck onto ranchers and their ilk, which then somehow metastasized into McMs before very long thereafter. And wouldn't you know it, *re-re-re-revivals* then emerged, closer to the end of the 20th, with somewhat more confident pastiches of bits appearing, on larger two-story houses for the most part. If that sounds like a McMansion, it almost is, but more to the point these might be considered McMs that have seen some, if by no means all, of the errors of their ways. For here those reliable revival styles were called upon yet again to get us out of hot water, in a trend aptly called "new traditional" in the *Field Guide* (Fig. 4.13).

More recently, architects have responded to a market for often expensive but, at last, in some cases, quite historically sort-of-correct designs. On the evidence, we have only to wait out the day when a *re-re-re-re-revival* comes along, edging us even a bit closer to confident stylistic usages. These may even include several sorts of modernism, for the origins of those so-called modern styles – which, again, is what they also are – have, after all, now been around for a century. And regional differences – what might be called vernaculars – are seeing an increased rediscovery as well, even though suburbia has spent the span of its existence attempting to destroy those very regional differences. Vernacular-based designs have characterized some "new urbanist" projects, the example of Seaside, Florida seeming to have sparked a revival, or more of an invention, actually, of a sort of upscale, low country cracker cottage architecture (Fig. 4.14).

All that said, it's encouraging that historicism in residential design is being applied at least a bit more competently, and it also bears noting, in terms of the single-family house generally, that there has always been good work done: it just gets shouted down a bit by the bad stuff. A measure of "complex simplicity" – meaning an overall simple design approach but one infused with incident and variety – might be considered a worthy goal, though a difficult one to achieve, accounting for why it shows up so seldom. Too simple, and a house (or any building type, really) is simplistic, boring; too complex and it's a thicket of unharmonious bits and pieces (*à la* the McMansions).

4.15
Starter homes.

4d. Smaller Houses in the Burbs

Much sound and fury having been expended herein on the McMansion and its ilk, it's only fair to turn one's attention to smaller houses of current and recent times; after all, it's a rather limited demographic that can afford the questionable judgment to McMansionise. There are lots of smaller homes for the smaller budget, though they often also aspire, rather futilely, to the McModel and its image of "gracious country living." But in the case of a starter home – the young couple having bravely moved up from the apartment to something barely detached – it seems that little in the way of graciousness can be afforded among what is on offer (Fig. 4.15). A not uncommon version of the not so big house gets the deserved sobriquet of a "snout house," wherein the requisite two car garage not only takes up more than half the façade but thrusts proudly forward, resulting in neighborhood enfilades consisting of little more than garage doors (Fig. 4.16). This happens because the garage remains firmly embedded in the front of the house rather than being detached and facing an alley instead, as was once the rule rather than the exception in such developments.[9]

---

9   Is the entry experience from the garage into the laundry room really preferable to a brief trip back outdoors via the back yard? Evidently, yes, and one can't really gainsay the advantages of avoiding such a trip in rain or snow, even though the attached frontal garage is perhaps the biggest stain of all on the recent domestic streetscape. Some recent developments would have a two-car garage facing an alley while featuring an accessory dwelling unit (ADU: for mother-in-law, rental, etc.) on the floor above: this idea, codes permitting, sweetens the pot of that approach.

4.16
Snout homes.

Private Life in the Burbs

4.17
Craftsman redux, Farmhouse, Contemporary.

Of course, style remains a subject of interest, with "craftsman" and "farmhouse" designs having grown in popularity, and it's fair to say this is a good thing, at least sometimes. But stylistic excesses remain, as in some over-decorated "Victorian" or Spanish Revival models, their reliably good features having often been misapplied. And then there is the style of modernism, for it is a style as well, and not the manifest destiny of all buildings henceforth as some schools of thought would have it (Fig. 4.17). Modernism has its roots in singular structures, sculptural objects on display in the garden, and just doesn't adapt all that well to ensembles, which is what houses in the burbs are, being lined up in rows. We speak not of mid-centuryism with its sheltering low-rise gables, but of the requisite modernist signatures of flat or shed roofs, appliqued siding in very light and/or very dark and neutral tones, and large areas of glass: difficult, really, to get right per se, not to mention in a context of more of the same.[10]

Again, often enough the floor plans for these smaller places cling to McMansion aspects, such as a fat footprint that leaves half the interior largely in the dark. Pointless 45-degree angles may also plague the layout. Sometimes there will be "vaulted" or "tray" ceilings, which will require custom framing both for the ceiling vault and the roof above, added costs among the many which account for the sticker shock level of recent, presumably modest single-family housing. Two stories are not uncommon among such smaller houses ("smaller" being a relative term), and given the typically reduced width of the site, proportions in front can get a bit teeter-y. Taken to extremes, as things always will be somewhere, they can get downright bizarre (Fig. 4.18).

4.18
Some extreme narrow housing (in Chesapeake, VA).

---

10   Realtors call recent such designs "contemporary," relegating the term "modern" to those of mid-last-century.

4.19
Narrow plan footprints compared: 40-foot lot, Zero-lot-line, Zero-both-lot-lines. For the sake of consistency, all of these feature garages to the rear, though some such houses locate the garage in front, rendering them sort of the ultimate in snout house design.

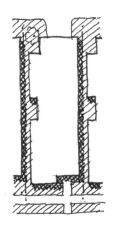
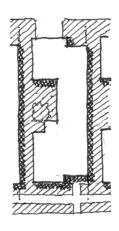
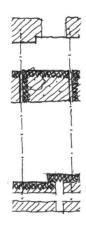

Such extremes aside, there is indeed a trend to narrow lots, with widths down in the 40-foot range. It's actually a trend that harkens back to typical neighborhoods of the '10s and '20s, before Levittown, and then the rancher came along and lot widths doubled and then tripled. Side yards thus rendered unusably narrow, the only outdoor areas remaining are in front and in back, although nowadays it seems many of those have shrunk to almost nothing as well! A better resort if narrow lots are to be the rule would seem to be the zero-lot-line house, which can incorporate a sort of off-center central courtyard in competent design hands. Or the lot lines may simply become zero on both sides, so to speak, resulting in attached housing, perhaps with a courtyard now separating the house from the garage facing an alley (Fig. 4.19). If two or three floors are involved, terrace housing (as the British call it) or what we call townhouses is the result. All of these, one may tiresomely note, are likely to be prey to some of the same sad foibles of cladding, trim, columns, windows, etc. as the McMs.

In response to colliding economic trends, the next step in the great shrinking of the single-family house finds it getting smaller on all sides, resulting in subdivisions of 600 and even 400 square foot houses, often garageless. Considered a snug but livable size for apartments abroad, these may seem to have reached the practical limit of a freestanding dwelling in this country (4.20). But extremes coming to extremes as they will, such developments with houses smaller and smaller yet have ultimately led to the "tiny house" trend: stick-built houses that are even smaller

Private Life in the Burbs

4.20
A dystopian subdivision of smaller-yet houses.

than single-wide mobile homes11 (Fig. 4.21). These range from the sleekly and all too cleverly ingenious to the well-intentioned and clumsy. They can even be equipped with wheels and, it is claimed, be towed down the highway to new locales. If indeed designed to be road-worthy, they tend to be taller than they are wide. And, their occupants may well want someplace else to go to on occasion that's not too far away, when the walls, already so very close, begin to seem to close in further.

---

11 The ultimate case of a smaller habitation, being none at all, is the fate of a great many homeless in the home of the brave. But the subject of tiny houses finds itself presenting a tiny but encouraging development in terms of compounds of super-small homes for the qualifying homeless. These may not even feature bathrooms or kitchens, those amenities being communal, but they are a step up from nothing. Although with 600,000 or so homeless it will take a while to house them this way.

4.21
Some "tiny houses."

4e. Buildings with Many Bedrooms

While a bit odd, that title seemed less awkward than "apartment buildings, retirement homes, dorms, motels, and hotels." This diverse cohort does have that attribute in common, and as a result there is something of an architectonic commonality among them, despite the widely differing ages of their occupants, if nothing else.

4.22
Typical three-story apartment building.

Apartment Buildings

Our focus here is what may be seen in a regular city or town, often at the seam between residential and commercial suburbia. (They are also found in downtowns, but their high-rise scale in that context can seem a bit removed from our present focus.) One durable prototype of the lower-rise apartment building is the layer cake of three floors of flats (Fig. 4.22). These may be variegated architectonically with an assortment of gable ends and bays and whatnot, or they may be flat as a pancake. Long-way gable roofs are the rule, though flat roofs are by no means unknown. Each of two basic layouts entails inevitable compromises: full depth units can mean open stairs in gloomy and drafty gaps, while a double-loaded approach means no-man's-land corridors, plus shallow, single exposure units.

A recurrent issue with such generally elongated buildings is the perceived need to break them up somehow, and as with so many things it seems difficult to avoid the extremes. One extreme might be an orderly march of repetitive elements in a dutiful expression of the indeed identical conditions that exist behind the façade. Projecting frames a bit like sideways TV screens is a sometimes-favored motif (Fig. 4.23). The other extreme, sometimes to be found in developments that closely define a street wall, involves changing the appearance of every unit in the row resulting in a jarring potpourri. Superficial façade variables on otherwise identical façades — brick veneer instead of siding, differing colors, "balconets" on some windows — fail to fool us. (Balconets, also called Juliette balconies or French balconies, are balconies with little or no depth and no floor either: stage-setting only.)

Private Life in the Burbs

4.23
Honest modernism
in apartment buildings.

4.24
A five-over-one.

In between lower rises and higher rises, there appears nowadays a wildly proliferating middle-height building type generically referred to as the five-over-one (Fig. 4.24). These arise from adjustments to building codes permitting five stories of all-wood matchstick construction stacked above a concrete-framed ground floor. The scale benefits to the developer are clear, and we now see these massive, chunky buildings everywhere, the unsolvable challenge of their visual-field-filling elevations a rebuff to the efforts of architects everywhere. That said, it bears noting that a building type of virtually contiguous five- or six-story street wall-defining apartment buildings is to be found in cities throughout Europe, and these generally have convincing or at least inoffensive urban qualities. They have been the rule there since the 18th century. And it's also true that rows of townhouses are a reliable housing type in places like Philadelphia and NYC, aggregating into block-long buildings. One thing that often sets these new ones apart is an excessive breaking-up of the façade into busy patterns. For another, as opposed to serving as street wall definers, 5+1s are often treated more like object buildings, in the long and undistinguished tradition of look-at-me modernism. And as massive, overscale object buildings of an edgy persuasion, they feel a bit like they're coming to get you.

Having edged ever closer from the suburbs to the middle of town, one may note a type of downtown retrofit wherein some late 19th/early 20th century commercial and warehouse buildings, lined up side-by-side on a street exposure, have had their upper floors converted to apartments or condominiums. These sorts of buildings are almost always far deeper than they are wide, so there is a fair amount of footprint in the middle of those upper floors (excepting skylight or clerestory opportunities on the top floor) that will have no access to natural light or natural ventilation. That's where we often see the bedrooms with no windows. One may dimly recall building codes that prohibit bedrooms without windows, but it seems there are now workarounds for that, and not only are these dark dungeons somewhat legal, but occupants say they like them for their isolation from street noise and daylight. Who knew! But what, you may say, of the correspondingly narrow and deep townhouses and apartment houses in places like Philadelphia and NYC? Well, it's a matter of scale, those blocks being shallower and having significant open space down the middle, making bedrooms without windows much less likely.

Retirement Homes

Who knew that an online search for "retirement home architecture images" would find an almost exclusively modernist cohort? Are the retirement homes, villages, communities, resorts, etc. in your town spiffy and sleek in their modernism, flat-roofed, and hard-edged, all? Around here they tend to be gable-topped, brick clad, and, often enough, festooned with classicizing furbelows, as if the aging aspire to eat cake alongside monarchs reigning therein. Some entry halls feature chandeliers and grand sweeping staircases, surely seldom to be ascended by the walker crowd (Fig. 4.25). But having raised a skeptical eyebrow at such high-browing, a basic goal of making such places residential in character, if just not quite so upper-crust in nature, surely seems reasonable enough.

Sometimes, though, it's almost as if residential character is being avoided, as if the management figures the users are fed up with a lifetime in residential surroundings and long for something more exotic. A pertinent note in this respect concerns the "senior living continuum" where the author's parents spent their last years, although it didn't used to be called that. A recently arrived mass mailing showcases the simulated

4.25
Grande retirement living (Florida).

"main street" inside their latest new building, the ceiling an assortment of gypboard vaults, the walls a cavalcade of Dryvit faux storefronts (and is that brick? You can't quite tell, given the wonders of modern fauxness). Some doors perhaps lead to the Unique Dining Options, some clearly don't open at all. (In the discussion herein of "Shopping Malls," perhaps it was a little optimistically precipitate to have promoted the merits of an interior "downtown streetscape concept" after all.)

The foregoing may seem to be simultaneously critical of both the modern and the traditional as appropriate settings for the aging, but such is intended only as regards the inappropriate application of either. This begs the question of what such appropriate settings might be. Well, it seems obvious, but large windows, ready access to the outdoors, abundant plant material, well-defined but interesting spatial sequences, and unbusy, colorful (but not too colorful) finishes would be a start. Let's get away from the funeral home look-- it's not time for that, not just yet.

Dormitories

Those who have gone to college — and nowadays so many have, whether well-suited for higher education or not — may have had the experience of dwelling in dorms. Generally, the main merit of these will have been to experience the expansive sense of free will bequeathed when one has *moved on* from dorms to off-campus housing, despite the likelihood that the latter will have been to a hovel, a firetrap shoehorned with several others into an aging Victorian era house that deserved better in its declining years. Like the several other building types that make up college campuses, dorms are not quite what you would call everyday architecture, but some aspects deserve our attention in the present context.

The basic interior organization of dorms divides roughly into earlier 20th century vs later. Earlier, double loaded corridors were the norm, the (usually double) rooms lined up, the toilets and showers down the hall. They were, of course, single gender, no other option being remotely conceivable in those days, those days being the early '60s and earlier. There would be lounges and study halls and maybe a cafeteria where the food was roundly and justly criticized. Later, the innovation of the suite came along, each with a small mix of single and double rooms and a small lounge and small toilet and shower rooms and maybe a small kitchenette. Well, each have their merits, but some may say the suite approach involved just a bit too much togetherness and smallness, while the earlier model allowed, rather ironically, for more flexibility and more varied personal interactions.

Those earlier dorms had a higher probability of having been designed in something like the "Collegiate Gothic" mold, though the interiors, possibly excepting the entrance hall, the lounge, and the dining hall, will have turned out to be pretty utilitarian in nature. More "modern" dorms will have run the risk of being pretty utilitarian on the exterior as well, lacking the compensating frisson of dear old Oxbridge to be had with CG. And given the attendant ambiguities of what constitutes currently accepted modes of modernism, it's no wonder that new dormitory buildings can seem difficult to get right.

For a number of reasons, on-campus dorms have been finding themselves in competition with off-campus condominium developments. The latter permit Daddy to make a speculative investment, which he cannot with dormitories, and it allows the student to adopt a dissipated lifestyle free from on-campus oversight. A cynical win-win all around, including for the developer, whose hastily built condos often do no favors for the neighborhoods adjoining campus that they encroach into and, in some cases, destroy.

Motels and Hotels

In nostalgic design terms, the motel's heyday was back before the interstate system destroyed long-distance motor travel. Well, of course it improved it by making it faster, but it simultaneously destroyed it by leaving behind all the well-established inns, eateries, and attractions of the old US highway system, offering featureless and soul-destroying routes in their place. Auto courts, cabins, cottages, camps — little lined-up individual structures — are fondly remembered for their rustic or quirky character, if not their solidity or amenities (Fig. 4.26). The archetypal motel arose from the inescapable logic of attaching these little buildings together into characteristic long and low profiles. A swimming pool was, if not a must, desirable; sometimes a lunchroom as well. The crowning glory was the neon-enhanced sign beloved by early modernism fans everywhere, emblazoned with flamboyant arrows, stars, boomerangs, and the like (Fig. 4.27). The Holiday Inn sign is a familiar example, though not an especially good one.

The ascendance of Holiday Inns and their ilk leads us literally to the next level, being the second-floor walkup. Its outside balcony corridor was direct, self-explanatory, and economical, having the sole drawback that everyone walks right by the windows, so the drapes are generally drawn. (To be sure, this hardly differs from the similar condition of earlier one-story motels.) Further expansion of the concept and its capacity sometimes found the balcony corridor on the other side as well, the building having become sort of double-loaded in reverse. Somehow these expansions of the archetype pared away some of the innocent appeal of a roadside idyll, making the coarseness that may have always been there a bit more architectonically evident, the stage thereby being set for the next step in what byway hostelries would become.

There's a not very well-defined distinction between motels and hotels; in fact, one shades into the other, the main distinction seeming to be that motels are smaller and cheaper than hotels. For our purposes, a motel refers to the sort of thing that has cropped up more and more over the years along the interstate, as opposed to the higher-rise downtown or the fancier resort version. There they are, out there along the bypass; indeed, who does stay in all those Springhills, Courtyards, Homewoods, Embassies, Best Westerns, Red Roofs, Motel 6s, Hamptons, Qualities,

4.26
A kabin kourt.

Private Life in the Burbs

4.27
Crowning glory signage.

Drurys, Residences, Hilton Gardens, Knights Inns, and Days Inns? Each is remarkably similar to its fellows elsewhere, arising from design standards set by the central office, and they recall architect Charles Moore's inimitable critique that "they weigh the tired traveler with the hopelessness of driving all day to arrive at a place just like the one he started from."[12] They're carefully pitched for their respective market segments, some on the cheaper side, others aspiring more to lugzury. In descending segmental order, there may be a sit-down breakfast menu not included in the room charge, a free hot breakfast buffet, or cellophaned sweet rolls and coffee in those "Bunn" warmers. There's usually, but by no means always, a chain restaurant nearby, and maybe a liquor store, and almost nothing else of interest. Perhaps there are not all that many front desks among such places that are behind bulletproof glass, such as one the author once encountered on a business trip, but these do exist and speak of security issues attendant to serving the unknown public daily. One does hear horror stories about disgraceful behavior on the part of hotel and motel guests which can tend to leave one with a bit more tenuous a grasp on respect for one's fellow man, sort of like the way you felt having read about the people on airplanes who fought with attendants when asked to put on a mask.

Of the architecture, these motels are overwhelmingly of the double-loaded corridor type, thus having replaced the slightly scary outside corridors with slightly scary inside ones. For a long while, their roofs were flat, but at some point the inevitable desire to set one's longish thinnish building apart from the competitors' resulted in some fishy efforts to apply gabled façade pieces onto what remained a flat-topped effort: these fooled no one

---

12   From "You Have to Pay for the Public Life," *Perspecta*, 1965.

4.28
Interstate hotels: flat roof, pitched roof, flat roof redux.

though one expects few cared. Then the difficulty of justifying an attic where none was needed was evidently overcome and a roofscape of low-profiled gables and hips became the new normal. In more recent days, things having come full circle as they often do, we find flat roofs again in the ascendant, perhaps with a fashionable "collided boxes" motif on the exterior to change things up a bit (Fig. 4.28). A recent exterior treatment of lesser merit has involved applying differently colored ribbons, panels or elbows, usually made of the ever-versatile Dryvit, to "break up" or "articulate" the exterior's still apparent boxiness. Clearly any significant departure from the basic rectangular solid has become difficult to justify, and something like this seems, lamentably, to be what motel architecture has become.

Other Sorts of Bedroom Buildings

Single room occupancies (SROs), boarding houses, prisons, YM- and YWCAs, hostels, and micro apartments aren't quite one or another of the above, but they are all also made up largely of bedrooms or living units in rows. They each have their separate reasons for being (though boarding houses, sadly, are largely a thing of the past), as well as their evolution through time as building types. Lacking distinctive architectural qualities to make an issue of, perhaps their mention alone will suffice here. Although one might note in passing the ironic problem of prison architecture, for while prisons do need to be designed somehow, there's generally an apparent wish to not make them too nice. One supposes it just doesn't seem suitable to make them pleasant, which could, in a limited way, certainly be done if we tried. But the prison system in this country is, after all, focused firmly on incarceration and punishment. You would think that having the largest percentage of imprisoned citizens – in fact, the largest number of prisoners, period – of any country in the world would make for a mighty sophisticated system: one which is at least doing what it can to prevent them from coming back. But, indeed, the opposite is the case, our prisons often being hellholes of violence where inmates learn new bad habits to join the ones that landed them there. Sentences, including those for victimless crimes, are often draconian, and the legal system is largely one of little more than back-room deal making. Some European countries have prison systems that emphasize rehabilitation, of all things, but it seems we can't be bothered very much with that in the land of the free.

4f.
"Mobile" homes

You would think mobile homes (MH) – once called trailers, now sometimes called "manufactured homes" – would be ideal grist for this sort of mill. And indeed they are, but for fewer reasons than were once the case. Anyway, for the sake of convenience if not accuracy, let's just keep calling them mobile homes. Our subject is the wide load item that is actually mobile only once, as a general rule, since only one in 10 is ever moved from its initial resting place. Mobile homes were once designed to be, well, mobile, in that they were a little more like today's caravan, though not as well constructed. Once the standard devolved to something that was meant to be trucked to a site and left there, the construction materials and details adjusted accordingly (Fig. 4.29). Such details are a bit hard to come by, but the general drift has it that in those days they were significantly less satisfactory than those of a corresponding site-built house. The industry claims that since HUD applied some standards in 1976, these aspects improved and became more thus comparable, but it may have taken a while for this to remotely be the case.

Perhaps the reader has seen the roadside tableau, peculiar to the south and to Appalachia, of an abandoned single-wide, kudzu covered and rusting. Mobile homes are more prevalent in the south, and so are hurricanes and tornados, which have a way of blowing them over or into the next county. They also go up in flames pretty fast on occasion, their occasional use as meth labs having been thought to have been a possible connection in that regard.

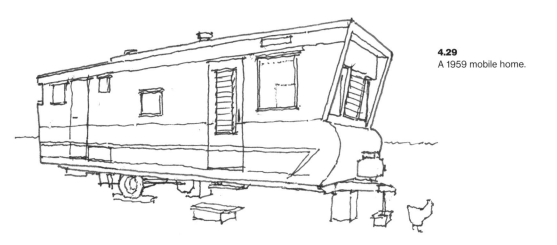

4.29
A 1959 mobile home.

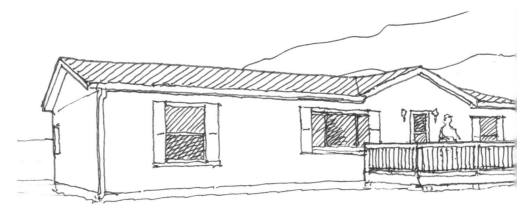

4.30
A modern-day mobile home.

To be fair, what of the pros of a mobile home? Well, they're cheaper, and get built fast, but advantages beyond those seem hard to come by. Well then, what of the cons? An industry scandal that persists to this day arises from the pervasive practice of renting the land one's mobile home resides on. Owners, strapped for cash for a number of reasons, which will have been among the reasons for having resorted to buying a mobile home in the first place, can find themselves evicted from the small patch of land their MH sits on due to an inability to keep up with payments thereon. And mobile home parks, mostly owned by large national companies, are mostly set up to rent the land.

The MH is more like a car than a house. One may say this is counterintuitive — after all, cars are far more carefully constructed than either — but value-wise an MH is appraised like a car or a TV set or a dishwasher. As opposed to a site-built house, which generally appreciates in value, the value of an MH steadily goes down, just like a car's does. So aside from a house that loses value from day one on a lot that isn't yours, what else do you get with a mobile home? When it comes to the architecture — and it's only fair to critique a mobile home as architecture, since it is being sold as the manufactured equivalent of a site-built house — there are a number of, well, peculiarities to note. The MH is likely to still be sitting on a steel chassis, though the tow bar, axles and tires are usually removed once a foundation of sorts is in place. Again, standards have improved since mid-last century, but a mobile home still has a way of looking different from a site-built house, even a very modest one (Fig. 4.30). The proportions, even those of a double-wide, kind of give them away, as do the sometimes flimsy looking "skirtings" that hide what's left of the chassis underneath. Newer models have gabled roofs, but these are, shall we say, streamlined in profile, their proportions having mainly to do with economy and with highway clearances. Construction takes place in a big warehouse-like space over a period of a week or less, so things do indeed go together pretty fast, a schedule arising more from a desire for labor economies than a timely benefit to the buyer. Tales of times past, which may or may not have changed that much since, would have a good ol' boy atmosphere prevailing at the job site, with a fairly rapid turnover of colorful characters that will all have one or more finger joints missing and sport a variety of tats. (But the latter is nothing unusual nowadays, having inexplicably become a fully transcultural phenomenon of semi-permanent epidermal self-expression.)

For a long time mobile home siding was ribbed aluminum, a holdover from the days when trailers were trailers. This is, to be sure, a durable choice that is still seen on single-wides in "parks" in the less desirable parts of communities everywhere (Fig. 4.31).[13] They simply have a way of sticking around, despite the materials and finishes within gradually going the way such things do. In more recent decades, the aluminum, which has a way of

---

13 To be fair, recent times find parks for double-wides as well as singles in a variety of suburban locations, which may feature community buildings and pools.

Private Life in the Burbs

looking a little wavy and thin, has been largely replaced by vinyl siding, also a bit wavy and thin in appearance. For an additional charge, cedar or fiber cement siding are also possible, and can be presentable if detailed well, though that is a telling proviso. A popular wood-like siding choice is "texture 1-11" plywood, again a little on the wavy and thin side. Shutters, which do have a decorative function if no longer a physical one, are likely to be narrow, thin, and face-screwed to the siding.

    It seems appropriate to comment here on the MH interior as well, but in fact there is little to be said: inside, things are much as one might expect, with eight-foot-high ceilings, narrow hallways, narrow rooms and narrow trims. Double-wides (there are even triple-wides) are a bit better in this regard, with ceiling variegations and various added furbelows, but their existential nature is still kind of unmistakable: it largely remains the case that you can always tell if it's a trailer. The good news of sorts is that the industry is trying to improve its image, and is offering options such as "modular" homes that are designed to have permanent foundations and to be adaptable to the vagaries of local codes. The not so good news is that their apparent aspirational look is pretty much that of a bare-bones rancher, with little effort made to innovate in architectural terms, presumably because the industry believes its potential customers don't want that. Sad to say, they're probably right.

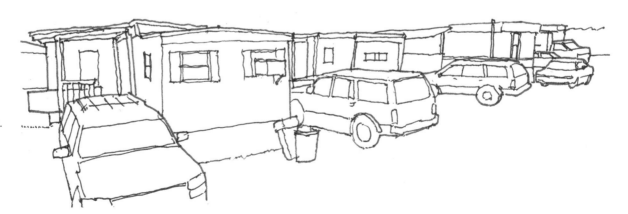

4.31
A mobile home park.

archit[ects]
on
the m[ove]

Design, good and bad, has as big a part to play with vehicles as with buildings: with the cars and trucks and whatnot that have come to so dominate the built environment. Homes away from home, they're everywhere and have their own foibles and environments.

ecture
ove

005

5.1
Once the Forward Look, now the Angry Look.

5a.
Cars and Their Domains

Why in the world would cars be included in a discussion of everyday architecture? Well, the latter phrase does mean something like "man-made constructions we get inside of daily," so in that regard you could say that cars qualify. Americans spend an average of an hour a day behind the wheel: they're a place of habitation. And the average car thus spends 23 hours a day sitting still and being available for admiration (or ridicule).

    Most everyone has an opinion of one kind or another about cars. Just as with non-mobile architecture, these may well include thoughts on quality, cost, and style. And while architecture buffs are likely, often as not, to be architects, car enthusiasts are everywhere. But there's a foundational thing about cars nowadays, and it's this: as a group, they're just not very cool anymore. Many are chunky, lumpy, and downright angry looking (Fig. 5.1). Maybe the wide-open mouth-grille with all the teeth and the squinty little headlight eyes are attempts to look cool, but they succeed mainly in looking terribly out of sorts.

    Cars, at least some of them, once seemed effortlessly stylish. One fondly recalls the debonair Studebakers and Kaisers, Chrysler's sleek (if flawed) "forward look" models, and the not-yet-eroded grace of the earlier 'Vettes and Porsches. Indeed, the best-looking cars ever made, though they were admittedly oh, so impractical, were roadsters. Everyone will have their favorites, such as the earlier Boxsters, Miatas (when they still had the flip-up headlights), the MGs, and the Jaguars (the XK-E allegedly deemed "the most beautiful car even made" by Enzo Ferrari) (Fig. 5.2).

5.2
The XK-E.

Architecture on the Move

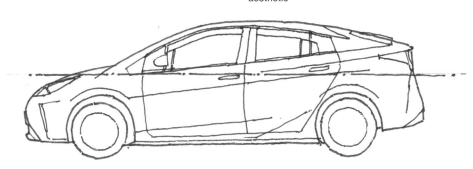

5.3
The tipped-down aesthetic

Flashes in the pan like the Avantis and Pacers, fine and not so fine cars respectively, were good-looking while they lasted. Readers, style experts all, will have their own choices for such a list. There's no denying that older production-line cars that were superficially stylish usually weren't very good in quality terms. That helped Japanese imports to help eviscerate the big old carmakers, the crash of 2008 providing the *coup de grâce*, and the industry in the US never really fully recovered. Style never really recovered either.

What happened to style, anyway? Did the advent of compacts and subcompacts inoculate the public against their cramped little interiors, driving everyone to minivans and SUVs?[1] SUVs have worse fuel efficiency than smaller cars, their higher center of gravity increases the risk of rollovers, their higher front-end profile makes them twice as likely to kill the pedestrians they hit, they give a sense of security that makes for less cautious driving, and their larger mass increases their braking radius, reduces visibility, and increases damage to others in collisions. But people feel safer in them (though they usually aren't), they have more room (which is often unnecessary), and you can see over the tops of the other cars (although many of the other cars seem to also be SUVs).

It may or may not be true, but it almost looks like the big, clumsy SUV infected the other car body types with its big, clumsy DNA: most everything has a sort of stubbiness now. Indeed, these stubby cars are remarkably similar in profile: at a glance, they all look just about the same, an optimized result of mass marketing, aerodynamics, government safety regulations, and internal space requirements for large people and their cargo. Perhaps in a failed attempt to compensate, we sometimes see the trick of tipping the side windowsill line and a crease in the side sheet metal downward going forward; maybe this is meant to make the car look kinetic and aggressive, but more generally it just plain looks out of plumb (Fig. 5.3). Perhaps the perceived stubbiness

---

1 And what's the real difference between the dimensionally similar minivans and SUVs, anyway? SUVs are more equipped for irresponsible off-road driving and consumption of fossil fuels: they're considered more "fun," or used to be. The SUV is marketed as more macho (it is simply bolted to a truck chassis, and don't we all want to identify with hard working real men who drive trucks and make $10 an hour) while the minivan ("mini": little, petite, feminine) as something the little woman could drive the little league team around in. The minivan is said to have more versatile doors and storage capabilities, the SUV more power train options for storming around fragile ecosystems. Body styles have evolved and variegated to the point that some SUVs now look a lot like sedans; there's even something called a compact SUV.

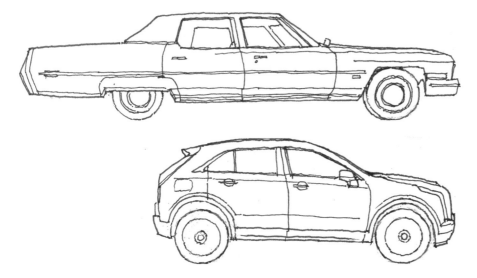

5.4
Lengths: '73 Cadillac Fleetwood Brougham (19+ feet); '23 Cadillac XT4 (15 feet).

of this century's cars arises, in part, from an unfair comparison with the glamorous lines of the '50s and '60s which, often enough, depended on absurdly stretched length dimensions of up to 19 or 20 feet (Fig. 5.4). All that said, some models actually seem to be rediscovering a sense of style generally, Tesla and Prius among them, so all is not necessarily lost.

Nearly since the automotive beginnings, headlights and taillights have been focal points for stylization. There was a time when headlights were round, and that's just the way they worked and they looked good that way, though they did look a little silly when ending up in pairs. Once HID and LED light sources joined sealed-beam halogens as options, weird-is-good headlight shapes became the rule. Ostensibly responding to aerodynamic optimization, the squint-eyed things have become the norm. Taillights have been stylistic wild cards for much longer, one fondly recalling the likes of Chrysler Imperial rocket ship taillights riding confidently atop the fins or collided therewith. The original T bird sported iconic round taillights, sadly debased in some subsequent models. But more recent years find taillight design having also lost its way, with a variety of amorphously shaped lenses floating around, artlessly chopped up for their assorted functions and either cut in two by the trunk hatch or squashed to the sides: too bad (Fig. 5.5).

Inside, nowadays one finds a cavalcade of instruments, buttons, touch panels, video screens, and gleaming little LEDs – or perhaps many of those elements have been incorporated into an overlord screen, where you may instead have the tapping-on-window glass experience you know and love from your iPhone. These items may signal the status of one or another of the over 100 computers installed therein, all waiting for the moment that they need to be turned off and on to see if that will fix them, except we can't do that. The car key is largely a thing of the past, though the enigmatic object that takes its place is equally susceptible to being dropped on the concrete. In many cars, an attempt to pull the bar under the front of the seat to move it forward or back will find that missing, all seat adjustments now being made from a witty assortment of knobs and toggles down alongside, none of which looks remotely like something that would do that. All these bits and pieces contribute to the current total of 30,000 parts per car.

It bears noting the obvious, that cars continue to be powered in the same basic way as they were at the turn of the last century, innumerable little hydrocarbon explosions driving the Rube Goldberg device that is the internal combustion engine, with its gaseous effluent continuing to drive up global warming. The advent of electrically powered cars offers a glimmer of hope, though the electricity continues to be produced, in considerable degree, by coal-fired means. That said, it's still an improvement, and the skeptical consumer may be impressed by macho-level acceleration potential and dramatically reduced fuel expenses.

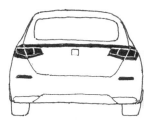
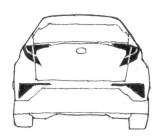

5.5
Some taillight oddities.
Clockwise from upper left:
Grumpy, Sleepy, Sneezy,
Bashful.

Car-Related Behavior

Car-related human behavior surely merits a glance, despite having almost nothing all that directly to do with car-related architecture. The many grievous things that people do while in their moving cars need not detain us; we all know what they are and we all know there is nothing we can do about them, infuriating and life-threatening though they often may be. But in passing, one might mention the habit of many drivers to drive from one adjoining destination to the next in the commercial suburbs. Bafflingly wasteful and lazy behavior on the face on it, this is the result partially of an environment tailored totally to the car, with a minimum of connective sidewalks and dangerous crosswalk situations that seem never to be used – or used solely by those without cars who have no alternative.

There's one thing that people do in non-moving cars that deserves attention, and that is sitting there in the car, in the parking lot, parked, with the motor running. This is to be found occurring in virtually every parking lot that one might try to park in: engines running for no apparent reason, in spite of the fact that idling is as atmospherically polluting as actually driving, if not more so. What are they doing in there, behind the often oddly dark windows, the motor purring away? Killing time before the next appointment? Perhaps. Putting off the dreary moment when they need to go home to the family? It's possible. But the most likely culprit is that they are in there indulging in their smartphone addiction. They've just spent 20 minutes behind the wheel or inside the Kroger and are thus behind schedule with their cellphone hits. The word is that users check in every 5.5 minutes, on average.

Their Domains

You may say something like don't blame the messenger, but cars are ultimately to blame for much of the flat-out ugliness of the suburban commercial landscape. Their view ahead enroute is dominated by three things: signage, road markings, and wires. Signs are enormous so as to be seen in the far distance by those approaching at 50 mph, and they appear in an endless enfilade that can make them hard to see anyway. Artless stripes and arrows decorate the pavement, while wires, poles, stoplights, traffic signs, streetlights, and more wires fill up the sky.[2] There are even skyscrapers, in the form of high-tension towers and cell towers, one or another of which will be looming in the distance. All

---

2 In fairness, this plague of wires is not directly attributable to car culture. It's attributable to our ability to tolerate such visual debasement, because to hide them in the ground or behind the buildings would cost more, and we can't have that.

that may seem to be stating the obvious – surely we all know all about all that – but it can still be revealing to take a snapshot of the suburban commercial environment, exposing the uglification that we have become blind to (Fig. 5.6).

While in the thick of a commercial connector road, one often turns out to be negotiating a largely contiguous 300-foot-wide pavement of moving and parked traffic, interrupted only by the minimal islands and buffers required by law. Shrubs may or may not be surviving in those conditions, and trees have a way of being few and far between. To be sure, every so often the main drag is greenery-buffered, and in those cases the 300-foot-wide pavements are off to the sides where they are surrounded by big boxes and little boxes (see "Shopping Centers"). It's even possible to drive, parallel to the main drag, from one parking lot to the next, on sort-of-default frontage roads.

Parking Garages

Once there are more cars than can be accommodated in parking lots, we get parking garages. Generally, these are no more attractive-- in a way they are even less so, rearing up to dominate the visual field with their bulk, relieved by no hint of human inhabitation. The most efficient parking garage designs turn out to involve park-on ramped floors, and unless these can be concealed in the middle – requiring a site that is over 180 feet wide – one side of a garage will slope, offering the exhilarating impression of partial collapse (Fig. 5.7). Parking garages present a challenge to innovative designers, and brave attempts have been made to turn them into "art objects," hard though that may be to visualize. Once they're built, they're hard to repurpose into anything else, something optimistic visionaries hope will be possible once car usage actually declines, given the assorted ramped floors and floor-to-floor heights suitable for garages and little else. In some high dollar parcels, on-site parking has been put fully underground, but this is very expensive, as is the constant forced ventilation required to keep them from filling up with carbon monoxide. More typically they rise up, with open sides permitting natural ventilation and views of many shiny grilles. Occasionally they've been tricked out to pose as office buildings with mullions in the "windows," but since these can't have any glass in them, the result tends to suggest the aftermath of a fire or a looting event. To give the due to some good practices regarding parking structures, if we must have them they can be buried in the middle of a block and surrounded by retail or residential. Or at the very least, the ground floors on street exposures can be lined with retail. And even if the site doesn't permit or call for functions other than warehousing cars, it's possible, given a sufficient budget and some ingenuity, to make a parking garage presentable, though this remains a bit of a long shot. (Fig. 5.8).

5.6
A car's eye view of commercial suburbia.

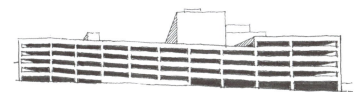

5.7
The appearance problem of park-on ramps.

Other Car Places

Cars have a way of generating a whole variety of further sketchy environments, which are pertinent to the topic of everyday architecture in their own particular negative ways. Car dealerships tend to be flashy and graphics-intensive, and used car lots take that to the next level with their carnivalesque pennants and blazing illumination. There are chain emporiums that exist to take your car off your hands for fully as much as half of what it's worth; if you're there, you may well be badly in need of funds to deal with some other exercise in bad judgement, or simply for being stuck at the wrong end of the American dream, as so many are. The ultimate sad fate of car togetherness outside the parking lot or the parking garage is the junkyard (they may call themselves wrecker services or salvage auctions) which every urban area features somewhere. And there are car part emporiums, that turn out to be junkyards for cars that have been deconstructed, and there are fair sized graveyards devoted solely to tires. At least someone is collecting them, though tires still have a way of showing up in the ditch or the creek or put to decorative use in planting beds.

Having glanced at these sad automotive end games, one feels obliged to make note of the perfectly legitimate and perfectly architecturally boring family of car care centers, auto parts stores, muffler places, oil changers, tire stores, car washes, and the like, but little more need be said other than that such places are thick on the ground, attesting to the utter prominence and dominance of the car in society. And these places need not be boring! They present widespread opportunities, so seldom exploited, for innovative design, evocative of speed (well, responsible speed) and style.

Clearly it turns out to be pretty easy to complain about cars and their domains, but ultimately they deserve a sort-of nod for their undeniable appeal in terms of freedom, style, and convenience. Once the frankly absurd internal combustion engine is finally replaced, cars will be hard to beat as the nation's conveyance of choice. And, the roads are already there, as opposed to the railroad system, which largely doesn't exist as such, through no fault of its own. Not to mention the propensity of cars to assist in cleaning up the national gene pool, though having pointed that out may be a bit too dark even for this commentary.

5.6
A parking garage designed for a conspicuous site on a Collegiate Gothic-ish campus, intentionally looking less obviously like a parking garage.

Everyday Architecture: A Vast Wasteland?

5.9
Some gas pump globes of yore.

5b.
Gas Stations

Back in the day when the single-family house sported revival styling, gas stations did as well. They were Tudor, Mediterranean, Mission Revival, Colonial Revival, and even sort of Georgian. But once the central place of petroleum in American daily life developed as such, the new idea of something called a "brand" came to pass and the increasingly ubiquitous stations came to be themed by their companies to encourage brand loyalty. Gas pumps themselves were wonders of singular design and graphics capped with internally illuminated bullseyes, shells, and crowns (Fig. 5.9). Oil companies went on to realize that it would be cheaper to simplify and standardize station design, so starting in the '30s the distinctive variations in roofscape that were central to the revival styles changed into the flat tops of box-shaped stations. In their defense, these often sported appealing design qualities, characteristically derived from art moderne precedents, and eventually the impact of the "international style" further streamlined these designs. They typically retained a certain up-to-date dignity, sometimes clad in sleek and durable baked enamel on steel (Fig. 5.10).

But bit by bit, an interesting building type became less so, although innovations could still occasionally be glimpsed. Eliot Noyes, an architect and designer of the elegant Selectric typewriter, also designed some of the most eye-catchingly modernist gas stations, their round canopies balanced on centerpoles (Fig. 5.11). Innovations of quite another kind had been cropping up since the '30s in the form of oddities with vaulted or hyperbolic paraboloid roofs, or in the shapes of shells, teapots, teepees, or airplanes. But these jaunty experiments were few and far between. By the '60s, box stations were sometimes remodeled and, along with new ones, designed in some vaguely historicist ("Colonial Revival") or residential ("ranch house") motifs. Thus, a full circle of a sort had come to pass, in passing, but not in a particularly good way.

5.10
Classic modernism in gas station design.

Architecture on the Move

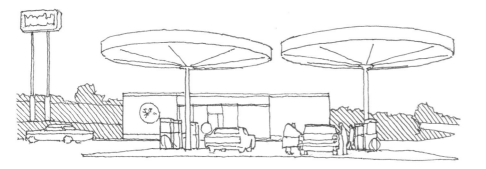

5.11
One of Eliot Noyes'
gas stations for Mobil.

Once the Interstate System became the way everyone drove long distances, whether they liked it or not, the attendant gas stations followed suit and basically became nonentities. Rather than the station itself, what one first sees is the pylon sign, or rather the cluster of many, each 50, 80, or 100 feet tall, all vying for attention. Then comes the looming canopy, capable of accommodating the shipping containers on wheels that now rule the road.[3] The unprepossessing boxbuilding beyond may have a flat roof, a "mansard," or a fake gable, but we really have no recollection because that structure has ended up becoming utterly unmemorable, a sad denouement for its sporty design history (Fig. 5.12).

Inside that boxbuilding, no particular attention has been given to design niceties and the only thing one really sees are the rank upon rank of every possible variety of junk food, flanked by the coolers full of every possible variety of sugar-infused, flavored, carbonated water, mostly of the 20-ounce persuasion, and what still sadly passes for mass-produced beer in the United States, ready to hand for one's convenience upon continuing down the freeway. (Speaking of convenience, some states have long had drive-thru liquor stores, as far as that goes, but that's another story.) Finally, the sales counter is positioned to protect the racks of otherwise easily stolen cigarettes, cigars, snuff, vaping devices, and paraphernalia for use in the consumption of illegal drugs. In addition to taking your money, the attendant sells lottery tickets, a popular item offering a chance at undeserved wealth sporting odds of 292 million to one or so. Once on a field trip to check out the design of courthouses, the author witnessed a judge avidly lining up for a couple of those.

At the pump we get to extract a credit card and insert it in the slot and then immediately remove it and immediately hopefully put it back where we found it (unless we must leave it there until TOLD to remove it). Perhaps, unaccountably, we must also enter our zip code, or our rewards code, though sunshine may well be rendering the digital information unreadable. Duct Tape (duck tape, if you prefer) may also be involved in the pump experience in one

---

3   Vivid shipping container imagery hardly does justice to the ever-growing length of 18 wheelers, for while the former is usually 40 feet long, the latter can be 80 feet long overall.

5.12
A present-day
interstate gas station.

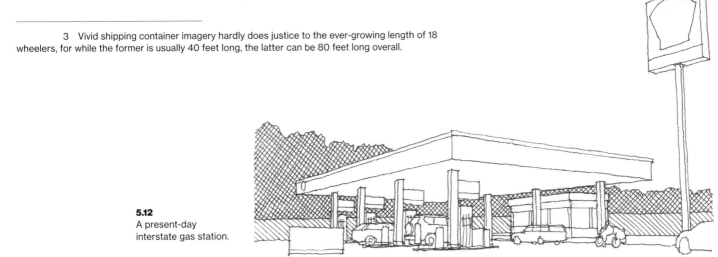

way or another. "Tap to pay" options at this writing may or may not include GooglePay, PayPal, Apple Pay, Chevron app, Shell app, Samsung Pay, Android Pay, Square Wallet, Visa Pay Wave, Venmo, Lifelock Wallet, or MasterCard PayPass: follow the seven steps carefully. Finally, be prepared to venture inside anyway should the pump end up telling you to "see cashier." Making a mindful choice of pump selection is important when diesel fuel is available there right next to the three gasoline choices. One must admit that the pump does have a helpfully long and flexible hose, but its ready use requires careful consideration on arrival as to whether the car's filler cap is located to the right front, right rear, left rear, or some other ingenious hiding place. The price of this petroleum byproduct is actually very low in view of the fact that driving creates all sorts of negative social impacts that aren't being compensated for, including lives lost to car crashes, personal time and productivity lost to traffic congestion, and health risks created by air pollution, to name a few. A more appropriate price of, say, $15 or so per gallon would probably not go over that well so the resulting deficit, like so many other deficits financial and societal, continues.

While waiting for the tank to fill, we may be unwillingly entertained by a local tv station's programming, emanating from a monitor built into the pump, filling a heretofore unmet need at the gas station for constant pseudo-factual input, perhaps arising from a generalized societal addiction to smartphone interaction. One thing we need not concern ourselves with is whether to let the attendant wash the windshield or check the oil, as these quaint services ended in the '70s, just as having him or her actually pump your gas for you ended in the '50s. But being Americans, we are self-reliant and tend to prefer doing things for ourselves.

One recalls that the gas station interiors of one's youth consisted primarily of the service bays, utilitarian places where work was done on the increasingly complex things that cars had become. Indeed, the two overhead doors that signified them on the façade were part of the iconic image of the gas station for a long time, along with the integrated canopy that floated forward. The service bays are now gone from current-model gas stations, dispersed instead to that armada of specialized chains servicing batteries, tires, brakes, transmissions, and the like, as well as to that whole other building type, the auto dealership. Dealing with wrecks, another inevitable auto-related subject, was also once the purview of the gas station, but nowadays there are whole car wreck specialists, not to mention the car wreck specialist lawyers whose tasteful billboards we all get to enjoy while on the freeway.

The gas station office of yore was just that, a modest place to pay for service, which sported a couple of vending machines offering the likes of Lance Cheese Nips and Co'Cola. A gumball machine may also have been in evidence sponsored by the local Rotary. If you're old enough, the Coke, Nehi, Grapette, and Royal Crown would have been in smallish glass bottles immersed in ice water in a chest cooler. But enough of such nostalgia; those days are long gone, and with them a sort of wistful innocence about car culture and gas station architecture.

5.13
Paris' Pompidou Center.

5c.
Industry

There actually is something called "industrial architecture," but it turns out to be just old mill and warehouse buildings that are being converted into lofts and offices. A more apt use of that term might be for newer buildings along the lines of Paris' Centre Pompidou, the influential modern art museum which celebrates the complicated "industrial flow" of utilities and of people up and down its outsides (Fig. 5.13). More generally, as we have seen, the popularity of what has been called "industrial chic" may similarly have arisen in part from a fascination with gadgets and things that move, or are expressive of movement: elevators out in the open, rolling doors, shiny round ducts, overhead doors, and ranks of wires and pipes.

But that said, what's mainly of interest here in the everyday are the actual forms arising from actual industry: grain silos and elevators, conveyor belts and hoppers of manufacturing and mining, drums and spheres for natural gas storage, distillation columns of chemical plants (Fig. 5.14). These forms have been admired by influential architects and artists, which is more than can be said for many of the other types of everyday architecture. Most of these forms also embody aspects of movement, thus their place here with other sorts of "architecture on the move," and they are expressive of what they do and little else, being engineered for particular functional purposes without attempts at decoration or enhancement. They don't need to be designed in the sense that is meant for the other building types; or rather they are designed in the engineering as opposed to the aesthetic sense. Their directness of form stands in bracing contrast to the inevitably multifaceted and often disappointing appearances of the everyday.[4]

While industry is different in this respect from our other building types, it remains an everyday sort of event, whether out in the countryside or right there in commercial suburbia, cropping up where terrain, access, zoning, and demand have facilitated its development. It's certainly true that industry can have its downsides, including atmospheric, olfactory, or sound pollution, and visual pollution as well should those interesting forms come with a shambles of construction and site depredation. And clearly the

---

4 Possibly of interest: the author's article, "The Artist, the Architect, and Industrial Form," in *The University of Tennessee Journal of Architecture*, Volume 7, 1983.

5.14
Some characteristic industrial forms: gas domes, conveyor belts, cooling towers, grain elevators.

office, lab, and storage buildings that are likely to accompany these industrial works may fall prey to the same prevalent aesthetic pitfalls as do all the rest.

    A special subtype of industrial form involves an important product that can't normally be seen at all: electrical power. Power plants, some of the nuclear type, may feature dramatic hyperboloid cooling towers, or ranks of very tall chimneys in the case of coal fired plants, those perhaps serving to move a plant's atmospheric effluent to the next state over. Past disasters – the near meltdown at Three Mile Island, or Tennessee's massive coal fly ash spill – have taken the edge off the romance of these commanding profiles. Electrical substation yards with their ranks of transformers, insulators, and wires may go by unnoticed, but they afford another ubiquitous case of industrial form, there being 55,000 of these throughout the US. And a final such manifestation, usually out in the country, is the hydroelectric dam. A double-edged sword, these dramatic structures generate electricity, impound water, and afford flood control, but sometimes do so at the expense of drowning scenic streams and their fauna, or even whole villages that ended up being in the way. Oh well, they were probably getting flooded all the time anyway; that seems to have been the rationale.

    So, industry is something of a wild card, largely experienced directly and day-to-day only by its workers, the general public seeing it when passing by enroute to somewhere else (or perhaps not really seeing it at all, which would be a bit of a shame). If its potential drawbacks are adequately controlled – to be sure, a significant criterion – industry can be a sort of ok event in the suburban scene: an inherently interesting building type that, for once, isn't all that encumbered with aspects of design gone wrong.

Architecture on the Move

5d. Other Architecture on the Move

The ice having been broken with "Cars and Their Domains," one may note that there's a motley assortment of other things that one gets inside of that move around: things that are likewise subject to design constraints, functionalities, and whimseys. But let's agree to the fore that some of these other media of transportation – buses, trams, railroads, watercraft, aircraft, spacecraft – are not everyday-architectural in nature. Well maybe they are, in some cases and respects, but we have to draw the line somewhere. True, superyacht design has some interesting extremities on offer, and there are some unusual aircraft designs as well, but the likes of those are really another matter.

Travel trailers

Travel trailers (not to be confused with "mobile homes") do qualify. They've been pretty funny ever since their origins, being an extended series of attempts to uproot a little homeplace and haul it down the road with you. Travel trailers have a rich and varied history dating back to the times when the cars to tow them first appeared, the more notable designs including spiffy little teardrop trailers dating from the '40s. And the Airstream line, having originated in the late '20s, set a high bar for construction quality and design excellence (Fig. 5.15). Caravans are the same thing as travel trailers, while camper vans are not; rather, the latter are the most basic version of:

Motor Homes

Also not to be confused with "mobile homes," these are basically the same thing as RVs, or recreation vehicles. But for that matter, travel trailers are also RVs. An unhelpfully all-inclusive term, an RV is anything that moves that is, well, recreational, while a motor home is distinguished from a travel trailer by virtue of having its motor built in. Both are available in a wide variety of levels of fanciness, ranging from basic – merely expensive – to something that can cost as much as a large McMansion. The "architecture" of both also represents a wide range of design quality, with many being slab-sided boxes featuring gaudy sweeping and swooping stick-on color schemes, dreamed up by designers who always wanted to work for car companies but didn't make the cut (Fig. 5.16).

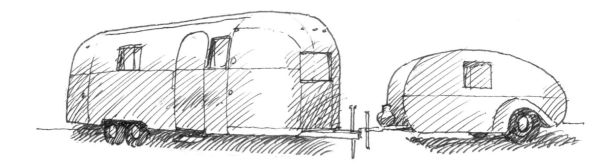

5.15
Airstream and Teardrop.

5.16
Sweeping and swooping.

Excepting those at the basic end, RVs come equipped with most of the comforts of home, boiled down to an ingenious lilliputian world in order to fit into something eight feet wide. Lengths vary from 21 feet to 45 feet, the same as school buses. Readers may differ, but the author hopes never to have to pilot a 45-foot-long vehicle down the interstate. "Pop-outs" may widen things a bit once the thing is no longer in motion, and other interior ingenuities feature transformer-like contraptions for turning banquettes into beds and the like. The more expensive the unit, the more circuits, switches, pipes, reservoirs, and computer chips there are for something to go wrong with. A familiarity with airplane restrooms will afford a preview of the sort of sanitary accommodation available – including a shower! – in the larger RVs, though perhaps not quite at that technological level, and one is forced to admire the resourcefulness with which these ultimate comforts of home have been dealt.

Trucks

From the style standpoint, truck enthusiasts may enthuse about a variety of fine points, but on balance trucks don't quite demand our attention in the style department the way that cars have. We are speaking here of those that are larger than pickup trucks, although some of the latter can be 20 feet long, a bit of a challenge for those 18-foot-deep parking bays in normal parking lots. While there is a wide variety of truck types – fire, concrete, tank, garbage, and so on – the ubiquitous tractor-trailer is our focus. The all-too-handy internet tells us that self-respecting TTs can be up to 65 feet long overall. Or 75 feet. Or 80 feet.[5] The thing with the engine and the cab is variously called a semi truck, a tractor, or a semi tractor, while the thing in the back can be a semi trailer (having back axles only), or a trailer (with axles in front as well). The full name of the front thing plus a semi trailer is a semi-tractor-trailer-truck, but it's easier to just call it an 18-wheeler, or a semi. But it can also be called a semi truck. One trusts all that's clear.

From the "architecture" standpoint, the thing in front may be the principal item of interest. "Cabovers," in use abroad but less so domestically nowadays, tend for some reason to be recalled with nostalgia by veteran truckers (Fig. 5.17). They have an imposingly compact profile with the engine partially below and partially invading the middle of the cab, and are praised for visibility and ease of steering, but not so

5.17
A cabover.

---

5   Something called "road trains," up to 175 feet in length, are permitted in parts of Australia.

Architecture on the Move

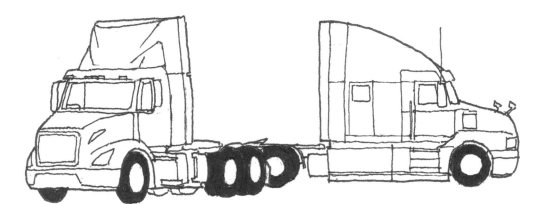

5.18
Cab with fairings;
a sleeper cab.

much for being loud, cold, and frontally vulnerable to weather and accidents. The flat cliff of the front face gives them rectilinear gravitas that the other ones, the "conventionals," simply don't quite have.

Those conventionals, emperors of the interstate, are called bonneted cab tractors in countries where hoods are called bonnets. The engine inside the bonnet is easier to service than a cabover's, which requires the whole cab to tilt forward, a dramatic sight which can look at a glance as if something's gone terribly wrong. Some other reasons for their popularity in the US are a smoother ride and improved aerodynamics, the latter further improved when ungraceful sheet metal "fairings" extend above the cab. While in earlier versions these tended to look a bit like the cab had gotten a pompadour hairdo, more recent designs are more convincingly integrated into the overall form of "sleeper cabs," that very space above and behind the cab housing a whole little microhome equipped with one or even two bunks, closets, microwave, refrigerator, TV, who knows what all (Figure 5.18). The biggest rigs of all can even have micro bathrooms. And Tesla has come up with a sleeper cab design that finally integrates that clumsy bonnet into a sleek overall shape.

The thing in back, the often rather flimsy and top-heavy trailer, reminds us of a similar shape that has become standardized in international trade, the shipping container. Most typically 40 feet long and durably made of heavy gauge steel, these have been put to alternative post-shipping use in commercial and residential projects, usually in combinations and with some number of openings cut in the sides. Results have been ingenious, though the attractive first cost of a used container can be rendered less so by the accumulated further costs of customization. Ironically, the design constraints imposed by the modular shape of these containers sometimes results in more convincing and eye-appealing results that is often the case with equivalent "stick-built" construction.

Just as gas stations are inevitable accompaniments to cars, so truck stops (or "travel centers") are for trucks. A car driver who inadvertently stops at one for gas may be startled by the small cities these have become, featuring restaurants, internet cafes, showers, laundries, service centers, truck washes, shops, endless aisles of junk food, and even fuel. There are rumors of short-term companionship being available at some truck stops but surely that is

5.19
Examples of art deco and recent modernist bus terminals (the latter, an aerial view, is sited on a bridge over connector roads).

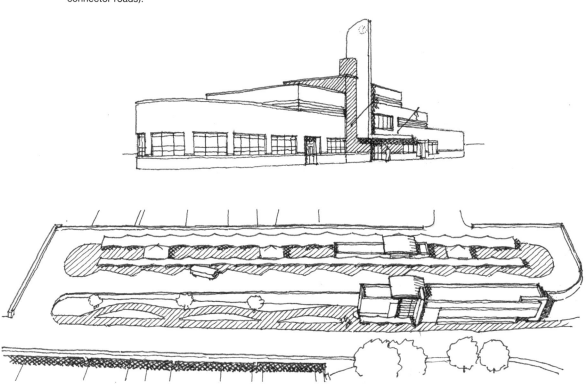

just hearsay. And as regards their architectonic merits, truck stops tend to be just as innovative as gas stations, meaning not so much.

As a travel center sidebar, we witness the growing phenomenon of travel centers for cars, the oddly spelled "Buc-ee's" appearing to be the largest. These are an exercise in having striven to expand both the gas pumping line and the adjacent convenience store to bizarre levels of hugeness, with 100 pumps or more lined up toward the horizon. Innovative architecture remaining a goal unsought, these installations depending instead on the impacts of scale and of a sort of comprehensiveness: they feature exhaustingly wide selections of soda (pop, if you prefer), candy, and beef jerky, among other healthful attractions. The spotless capaciousness of their restrooms is notable as well, perhaps due to the contrasting state of so many regular gas station conveniences.

Train and Bus Stations

As gas stations and truck stops are for cars and trucks, so then are terminals, stations, depots and garages for trains or buses or trams. Readers may be familiar with a grand version of one or another of these, such as Philly's 30th Street Station or NYC's Grand Central. Far from everyday, these are fine exemplars of public architecture writ large. More impressive yet was NYC's monumental Penn Station, its demolition in the '60s an act so egregious that it set off the whole architectural preservation movement. Also egregious was its replacement, a warren of dark tunnels and passages that was essentially the basement of Madison Square Garden, itself an arena building of no merit that inherited its name from another monumental landmark, also demolished. Moynihan Train Hall, a new replacement for Penn Station's train hall, is a partial renovation of NYC's former main post office building, and while expensive and impressive, it lacks the gravitas of the original. It's fair to say that train stations of all sizes tend to do a good job architecturally across the country, though there really aren't as many as you might think, at least not all that many in use as train stations. That would be due to the deplorable decline of rail service, due to the corresponding and inexorable expansion of, what else, car culture.

Bus stations also have a good record of architectural quality, either as spirited art deco or as sometimes-well-applied modernism (Fig. 5.19). But the way of life inside bus stations, and inside buses, can be, well, basic. Such buses are the LCD of travel, just shy of hitch-hiking, and those without much to spend on transit will be found there.

Airports

Like hospitals, airports are always under construction. Often flamboyant and disorienting, they are generally ill-designed to calm the always anxious air traveler. They're everyday enough in that every city of much size has one. As opposed to train stations, typically located conveniently in the middle of town, airports are of necessity way out there in the remote industrial or lower-income suburbs. Air travel, once glamorous, has become a bit too much like inter-city bus travel, and the airport is now likewise a bit too much like the bus station. Perhaps they will become obsolete when Elon Musk's tunnels are finished. By the time one has driven to the typically rather far-away airport to be there an hour and a half early and has gone through the petty humiliations of security, and then flown (hoping for no on-board altercations or fisticuffs), then taken the bus to the rental car place, and driven to one's destination, the wonders of flight may have taken as long as a corresponding train trip, if there were a train to take. And there's always the possibility of flights being cancelled due, among so many other possibilities, to bad weather. Nothing toughens up the hardy traveler like a string of thunderstorms cancelling everything, the hotel vouchers having been snapped up by others, and night descending, along with the airport restaurant and bar security grilles.

open space

Every one of those everyday building types has turned out to annoy us in some way or another, and we've found that the intervening streets and parking lots, which consume fully half of the space in our cities, are no better. But there are other types of open space, precincts of breathing room that can afford a measure of relief, even of pleasure, amid the wasteland. And urban open space, done well, will help elevate those everyday buildings.

6a.
Parks and Places Like Them

On the face of it, "open spaces" would seem to be well outside the purview of a book about architecture. But there are several categories of open space that are part and parcel of what makes up the fabric of urban and suburban development, and they have direct relationships with one or another of our everyday building types. And it does bears noting that they tend to come off a bit better than all those "built-space" types. The following concerns three quite different sorts of defined open space – that aren't parking lots – found in most cities and towns.

6.1
Ghirardelli Square, San Francisco: the old chocolate factory that anchors things dates from 1852, while the commercial development opened in 1964. Its spatial sequence remains hard to beat as an exemplar of urban open space design. Photo courtesy of Jamestown Urban Management.

Squares and Streets

A "town square" is something one might vaguely associate with smaller towns in less urbanized areas of the country, conjuring images of a leafy rectangular park with a Victorian era county courthouse in the middle. Many such places do exist, and towns that aren't county seats may still feature town greens, possibly centering on a gazebo or a war memorial. But beyond this pleasant model, there's no well-established American tradition for a central urban plaza corresponding to European precedents. Some so-called squares in American cities, such as Philadelphia's Rittenhouse Square or Savannah's Wright Square, are also actually parks, and while welcome respites in dense urban areas, they don't come off as (nor are they usually meant to be) urban plazas. Indeed, numerous cities and towns have no central square at all: a lively stretch of downtown street ends up being what many Americans think of as the center of town, though streets are, after all, primarily about cars. That said, we're glad to have such "main streets" and wish there was something like them in the

Open Spaces

commercial suburbs, where central spaces are likely to be nothing more than parking lots. Some streets can afford a desirable sense of place if provided with trees, attractive pavements, and amenities to serve pedestrians. Some have even been fully converted to pedestrian use and become "linear squares" of a sort.

Unfortunately, that nostalgic main street image doesn't jibe with the modern-day reality in some downtowns where a fair share of storefronts are empty, a fate largely due to those commercial burbs. To enhance their attractiveness as places to be (and thus their commercial viability), many of those main streets could use some sort of town square-like place to focus the middle of town further. But again, the town square tradition in America is really one of downtown parks as opposed to something more like the paved plazas, market squares, and pedestrian streets of Europe. One supposes it's partly our bad weather that accounts for this, though trees and shade structures can and do render paved plazas more livable. Paved plazas are more versatile for public gatherings such as markets and musical events, and some do exist, whether private, like San Francisco's Ghirardelli Square, or public, like Portland's Pioneer Courthouse Square (Figs.6.1 & 6.2).[1]

---

[1] Of possible interest regarding a comparison of urban squares in the old and new worlds: the author's book, *Urban Lessons of the Venetian Squares*, ORO Editions, 2022.

6.2
Pioneer Courthouse Square, Portland, OR. Opened in 1984, the full-block plaza accommodates a wide variety of urban amenities and events, though the large central space can seem vacant when large scale events aren't underway. Photo by Alamy.

Parks

Parks, in the more conventional sense of green spaces embedded in the urban fabric of cities and towns, are mightily important to the urban quality of life, though opinions will vary on what properly constitutes a city park. It's not uncommon for a community's parks-and-rec department to mistakenly regard a ballfield complex as a park, the former being about organized athletic competition as opposed to unstructured recreation and relaxation. (Well, yes, it is a "ballpark," but that's a matter of terminology.) Botanical gardens, arboretums, commons, reservations: all are types of parks, though some are public and some are private. In any of these, natural watercourses and ponds are usually considered desirable amenities, providing (as with all city park amenities) they are suitably maintained. *Artificial* water features should be undertaken in the full knowledge that they will require more maintenance than anyone will have foreseen, and will probably be shut down and most likely eventually demolished at some point in the future. And that they will probably be legally required to be surprisingly shallow, with hardly any depth at all, really. Indeed, nowadays we see the trend to zero-depth play fountains rather than actual pools, meant to defeat the most determined attempts at inadvertent drowning or aquatic peeing.

City park architecture is usually modest: gazebos, picnic shelters, restrooms, and changing rooms for the pool (municipal swimming pools continuing to buck the zero depth trend). Unfortunately, that modest scale often seems to bring a corresponding humbleness of budget and of design aspiration, and it's become a little too easy for the likes of bandstands and shade structures to come out of a catalog, with all the anonymity of appearance this is likely to entail. Playgrounds, also time-honored features of city parks, tend as well in recent times to have come from a catalog, and to be rather safer and thus rather less interesting from the play standpoint than in times past. But safety and accessibility are important, one must grudgingly admit. There may be a concession stand or some modest bleachers for a ballfield, but if the ballfields come in cloverleafed groups of four with centralized amenities, we are speaking of a ballpark rather than a passive park. That latter rather weak-tea moniker was dreamed up awhile back to signify parkscapes where the main attraction is, indeed, one of not doing much, and there's nothing wrong with that.

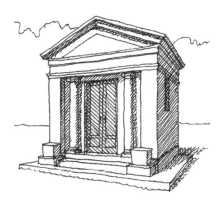

6.3
A Mausoleum.

6.4
A Headstone.

Cemeteries

Cemeteries are yet another kind of park. Their architecture, when in the form of individual mausolea, comprises what is perhaps the oddest of all building types: houses for the dead. Little of note (aside from the polite and quiet residents) is found within, for these are miniature edifices mainly meant to impress, as with McMansions in the case of the living. Greek Revival temples predominate, though Gothic and Egyptian Revival versions exist (Fig. 6.3). Alternatively, "apartments" for the dead make up the sort of collective mausoleum wherein crypts for caskets, recesses for urns, and plaques for names are choices afforded. These buildings are likely to be clad in those same revivalist trappings, though some nice modernist mausolea do exist. Well-known architects favor such a project, perhaps because the user group is in no position to raise questions about design choices.

A substantial step down in scale from the family mausoleum finds the ubiquitous gravestone or headstone. These usually end up as the familiar flattish upright objects, though from mid-20th century onward flat-to-the ground stones have become increasingly prevalent. While the latter are sometimes provided with handy receptors for flowers, sadly flowers tend usually to be supplied in the artificial variety, their enduring tackiness ironically undermining the presumed goal of a simplified landscape setting that flush-to-the-ground markers would afford. Given the lack of any design precedents to speak of, gravestone designers offer a variety of fanciful designs instead. Angels, shells, hearts, flowers – the perceived necessity of elaborating a simple graphic composition has led suppliers, who seem to have felt no compelling need to employ those schooled in the design arts, to give free rein to the imagination (Fig. 6.4).

While consuming a lot of acreage, cemeteries do act as green oases that provide a range of important natural habitats for many different plants and animals. Being relatively secure from commercial development, they afford large partially wooded areas that help to filter air and water, control storm water, and conserve energy. But cemeteries do have a downside: conventional burials use toxic chemicals that can work their way into the soil and underground waterways. Cremation is increasingly thought to be a better option to the sentimental preservation of human remains, the resulting ash presenting no particular environmental hazards. But the process itself generates harmful air pollutants and releases a lot of carbon dioxide. In light of these troubling outcomes of our conflicted approach to mortality, death having proven to be the fate awaiting most of us, one or another variety of natural or "green" burial is said to be gaining support.

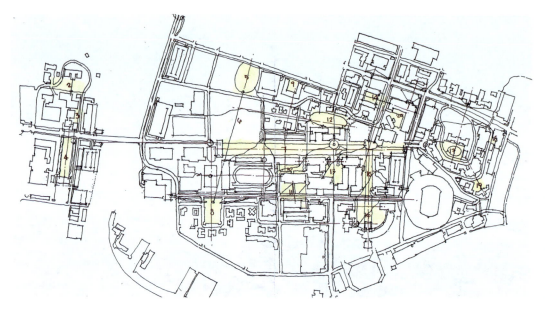

6.5
A preliminary study for a university master planning effort, showing a mixture of existing and proposed buildings. This dense urban campus still manages to be organized around quads, malls, and greens. (As is the way with master plans, this version is already well out of date.)

6b.
Campuses and Places Like Them

The following odd cohort shares a commonality, being groupings of multiple buildings, normally found in or adjoining cities or towns, that involve a sort of symbiotic relationship with multiple associated outdoor open spaces.

variety (Fig. 6.5). All this is to note the distinctive and leafy pedestrian-oriented role such campus open spaces play, in contrast to the typical urban spatial experience (the street) or the suburban one (the parking lot).

Universities

Colleges and universities across the country adhere, fairly consistently, to a "quadrangle" approach for the disposition of their buildings and open spaces. One can see precedents at places like Oxford and Cambridge where the buildings of the older colleges fully surround and define rectangular courtyards, thus resembling the cloisters of medieval abbeys. In more modern times such green squares are less fully enclosed by the buildings that define them, but the desirable sense of the outdoors as a "series of rooms" prevails, at least to some extent, some of the time. Greens or commons—larger open spaces with more irregular boundaries—are also to be found on the luckier campuses, as are elongated, axial "malls," not to be confused with the suburban shopping

Military Bases

The US Department of Defense owns 30 million acres, found in every state in sometimes enormous installations. It's the world's biggest employer with the world's biggest military spending more than twice over. While military bases involve a measure of defined open space, sort of like college campuses do, the buildings themselves fail to measure up very much. As with prison design, attractive architecture often seems felt to be inappropriate, a bit namby pamby, for the no-nonsense attitude that appears to prevail regarding life on the base. Drab buildings at these places do little to enhance the experience, and some small measure of blame for the dysfunction one sometimes hears about regarding military life might possibly be assigned to these dispiriting environments.

Open Spaces

Fairgrounds

Fairgrounds are about as ubiquitous as campuses: two thirds of the more than 3,000 counties in the USA feature a fairground. While some are modest acreages, others are a pretty big deal, and state fairs are the biggest deals. Once lying rather fallow, except for a few weeks in the fall, more and more these places are becoming year-round events centers. As with campuses, a fairground features an assortment of buildings, but rather than libraries, classroom buildings, and dormitories, they feature arenas, exhibit buildings, and livestock barns. And instead of quadrangles, commons, and malls, they feature exhibit and midway lawns, amphitheaters, and livestock rings. So they amount to a lot more than the carnival, though that's the main attraction for a good many visitors. Planning a fairground can be a significant exercise, just a bit like planning a college campus except with livestock involved and with lower budgets (Fig. 6.6). Fairground architecture has to deal with the challenge of its image – that these modest structures need no particular design attention – when in reality they need more than usual in order to overcome the often prevailing limitations of pre-engineered building systems, modest budgets, and modest expectations.

6.6
Some examples of concept-level fairground master plans for sites in Texas, California, and Illinois. All feature well-defined central open spaces.

6c.
Sports in the Outdoors

One might classify sports as entertainment, though recreation would probably be a better term, ultimately, both apply. (Pro sports teams are a different animal, being also a business.) Anyway, we speak here of sporting facilities that are out in the open: baseball, football, soccer, tennis, golf, track, and the rest. This assortment is certainly a ubiquitous open space amenity in the burbs, and in theory it points to a healthful community interest in physical activity, although it could also be said to embody an obsessive and not invariably healthy interest in competitiveness.

And there is the whole building type of the public recreation center, featuring basketball courts, swimming pools, and the like, usually along with some outdoor sports fields. Given their diverse programs, these can be good opportunities for good-looking design, but often enough the largely solid-sided box housing the basketball courts turns out to have been too much of a challenge in that respect. Such buildings sometime feature an indoor running track overlooking the basketball courts and possibly continuing around adjacent fitness spaces, which will fortuitously contribute to a dynamic spatial quality even in the absence of much design initiative.

While golf courses consume large acreages of valuable property, they are probably better for the environment than what might be there otherwise. It seems a difficult game to those of us among the uninitiated (there's a little Robin Williams routine about that) making its popularity a bit baffling. Enthusiasts praise the healthful and stress-reducing outdoor exercise it entails, and the fact that the length of the game facilitates getting to know — or attempting to secure business relationships with–others. Golf course architecture is most visibly represented by that of the country club, and while it can be on the stodgy side, rather like some of the membership, it is usually pretty well done. Something might be said here along the lines of why is it that the good stuff is thus reserved for the well-off and well-connected, but ultimately if we must have such exclusivity, better it be done well than poorly.

And there are racetracks, though it's true that these aren't going to be found in every city and town. They may be for animal racing, including of the horse and greyhound varieties in the US, though there are only two of the latter remaining. There are a good many bicycle velodromes, and bicycle races also sometimes occur on city streets, resulting in maddening street closures for non-enthusiast residents, often enough. And there are racetracks involving armored, high-powered contraptions pretending to be cars. Types include Formula One ("IndyCar" in the US), with no pretense that the vehicles are anything but elaborate devices custom fabricated at enormous expense. But it is stock car racing--though these cars have also been greatly modified— as epitomized by NASCAR, that dominates the American auto racing sensibility.[2] It is a sensibility that is focused on the ever-present possibility of

---

2   The 2006 film "Talladega Nights" affords a dignified summary of NASCAR culture.

Open Spaces

6.7
Footprints of a high school track, the Churchill Downs track, and the Daytona Speedway track, all to the same scale.

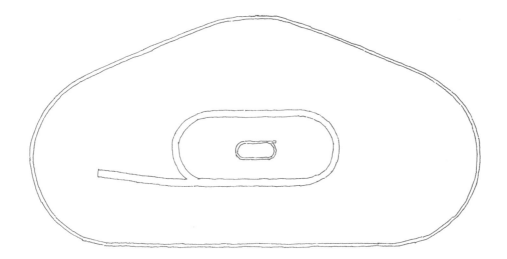

spectacular flaming crashes from which drivers almost always, incredibly, walk away. No one quite seems to know the total number of ovals, dirt tracks and drag strips out there but there's probably one near you.

Having gossiped a bit about these sports generally (research having confirmed that it is correct to call them sports), the architecture of racetracks deserves some attention. Louisville's Churchill Downs is known for its vaguely iconic twin spires, though bigger and newer grandstands now loom above them. New York City's Belmont Park once featured a massive roof over its grandstand attendees, and an even bigger cantilevered lid dominates the grounds today. Horseracing is not what it once was, though, any number of fairgrounds around the country having tried to figure out what to do with their obsolete tracks and grandstands. As for NASCAR grandstands, they offer little architectural distinction, comprising huge swaths of stands for huge numbers of fans, with the customary boxes for elites looming above (Fig. 6.7). The fan experience, including whatever it is that takes place on the infield, is said to constitute a good measure of hearing-damaging, alcohol-fueled abandon.[3]

---

3   The author once didn't quite get the job of designing a welcome center for the Daytona Speedway, but he was given one lap around the track (as a passenger).

6.8
An example of a roadway bridge over a freeway that exhibits some intentional design.

6d.
Open Space Gone to Waste

Arguably the sorriest category of open space in and around town is the space that's simply wasted. There's been more than one occasion herein to be offended by parking lots, and they are indeed remarkably wasteful, taking up over three times the space occupied by the cars themselves when full to capacity. One statistic offers that there are eight parking places for every car nationwide. Often enough, land use plans that compare downtown built-up areas to open space areas exhibit a dramatic change from 50 years ago, to the benefit of open space, in the form of parking lots.

We've also had occasion to criticize wasteful subdivision lot sizes in suburbia, notably in the way houses are plopped in the middle with much of the remaining property being notably unusable. This highlights the fantasy of living in a country estate surrounded by rolling countryside, an English one to judge by the prevalence of British-style subdivision nomenclature. Such subdivisions may come with grand entrances, featuring signage, lighting, lavish landscaping, and elaborate masonry — sometimes even little unmanned gatehouses — comprising more convincing design efforts than do the houses themselves. In some cases, the ultimate feature of such gates is actual gates, openable via a keypad or fob and rendering the subdivision a "gated community." While presumably offering some increased measure of privacy and security, these also have a way of not so subtly enhancing the polarization of modern society.

Highways waste a lot of space as well, as in excessive numbers of lanes, excessive median widths, and the special requirements pertaining to higher speeds. A classic case would be the acreage entrained by cloverleaf-style intersections, dooming those spaces to no use whatever other than lawns and greenery:

Open Spaces

environmentally desirable, perhaps, but places no one can access or use. Sometimes the biggest structures in town turn out to be parts of freeways: bridges, retaining walls, sound walls, and elevated ramps. If well designed, these can be evocative of movement and travel, and good graphics and landscape materials will further enhance such civil structures (Fig. 6.8). Sadly though, these massive constructs will often show little or no design hand and are simply clumsy and obtrusive, ending up by aggravating rather than easing the driving experience. It bears noting that larger road and railroad bridges have the potential to be stirring examples of engineering art (the Golden Gate, for example). But often enough the driver experience on a bridge is little different from that on land, even to the extent that a view of the water is frequently obscured by solid parapets.

When freeways are enlarged, a typical resort in response to increased traffic congestion, something called "induced demand" tends to result in correspondingly enlarged traffic, cancelling out the presumed benefit of ever larger roads. Traffic planning dating back decades ago no longer suits urban planning that is better oriented to people, requiring expensive efforts to undo unnecessary or ineffective connector roads that consume valuable real estate and isolate one neighborhood from the next. Efforts are indeed underway to right some of these sorts of wrongs, with programs of freeway *removal*. Demolishing harmful and obsolete sections of freeway permits reconnected street networks and the development of mixed-use urban areas, parks, and other desirable land uses. (Google "Freeways Without Futures" if interested in this encouraging development.)

Finally, speaking of waste, it's unavoidably true that the massive amounts of trash we throw away has to go somewhere, so a lot of space gets consumed in the form of landfills.[4] Perhaps you've wondered what in the world it may be that a neighbor throws away weekly, perennially overtopping their 96-gallon trash toter. (For comparison, the author's daughter's family in England throws out nine gallons of trash per week.) Whatever it is, it joins mountains of residential and commercial waste in landfills, hidden away somewhere not far from where you live. In flatter parts of the country, these can be topographic landscapes of their own comprising the highest points in town. Landfills can be far from harmless, bringing the potential of odor, noise, smoke, and water supply contamination if not carefully developed and monitored. And their several types include those for hazardous waste, there being thousands of hazardous waste and "Superfund" sites and cleanups throughout the country. Low-income areas, with fewer resources to oppose landfill placement, are more likely to end up as home to landfills and hazardous waste sites. It all sounds rather depressing, and is. Fortunately, there's one more "open space" chapter that turns out to be a bit more upbeat.

---

4   Also characterized by heaps of waste material, the various sorts of surface mining are surprisingly ubiquitous scars on the landscape, out beyond the burbs and in them as well.

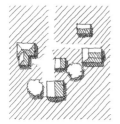 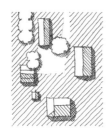 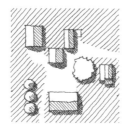

6.9
Some small farmstead complexes, seen from above. These examples, chosen at random, are all in the same general area in central Illinois. Devoid of symmetry or axial alignments, they consistently exhibit unintentional compositional balance.

6e.
Out in the Countryside

Found in the ultimate open space of the rural countryside, we've made passing mention of power plants, industrial sites, landfills, strip mines, and other such large-scale interruptions of the natural environment. But we also find a collection of some further building types that exist only here, removed from urban or suburban settings. And these strange bedfellows usually turn out to have redeeming architectural qualities, making them quite the exception to the rest of our everyday architecture.

In large parts of the nation, if you get out beyond the suburbs via non-interstate routes, farm buildings will soon appear. Vernacular tradition, along with simple utility, can result in a sense of apt fitness for these building groups.[5] Choices made over the years in the siting and expansion of such farmsteads, while likely made solely for functional purposes, almost always end up having some measure of artful interrelationship in their layouts (Fig. 6.9). Sadly though, the increasing prevalence of "pre-engineered" buildings on farms has blunted the appeal of these little (or not so little) rural complexes.

Another type of farmstead, sort of, would be the winery. Some have employed the skills of well-known design architects, with surprisingly random results as to their buildings' architectonic merits. Rural wineries can spread out, budget permitting, into whatever fanciful composition is wanted. And as with some of our other building types, such a relative lack of constraint can and often does lead to excess. (Excess can also be a factor in wine tastings, as in the popular trolley and limo tours of multiple winery locales.)

There are some other building types found in natural areas that notably involve professional design work. State and national park architecture usually represents a good effort, such projects sometimes sought after as high-profile commissions. And the public client, while sometimes inflexible, is at least usually motivated to do a good job as well. These buildings, ranging from welcome centers and lodges and cabins, to restroom buildings and picnic shelters, generally benefit from beautiful natural settings, as well as some fine precedents in terms of picturesque, vernacular-inspired design, Yellowstone's Old Faithful Inn being but one familiar example (Fig. 6.10). There was widespread construction of such buildings and civil structures in the '30s under the auspices of the Works Progress Administration and other such federal programs, setting an enduring high standard for such "rustic architecture."

Some such parks call themselves resort parks, and of course there are also places that are simply resorts. Not usually found in the city or the suburb, these have a way of being their own self-contained sort of townscape. They may focus on amusement (inevitably Disney comes to mind), or

---

5 In a beginning architecture drawing course, the author and his classmates were once told to get outside of town and find a farmstead and (as best as one could by visual estimation) draw up their volumes and spatial relationships. These layouts then served as a basis for delineation techniques, shadow casting practice, and the like, but also turned out to be surprising exemplars of artful composition.

6.10
Old Faithful Inn (1904), at Yellowstone National Park.

recreation (golf, spa, seaside, gambling). Unlike the national parks, they are often primarily places for the privileged and their wannabes, who bring with them the questionable taste in design that such places sometimes embody. It's fair to say that such resorts are meant to be the antithesis of the everyday for their patrons, though they do comprise a good measure of everyday life for their cleaning and maintenance staffs. The latter goes for hotels generally and, when you think about it, most of our everyday building types.

Finally, the interstate will, sooner or later, bring you to some interstate architecture in the form of welcome centers and rest areas. These vary rather more in design merits than do the park buildings, but they at least represent a stab at something or other. The wide variety of these places is understandable, there really being no particular precedent for how they should look beyond the available option of some vague regional imagery. In Virginia, they tend to be colonialesque, while further south a sort of subtropical overhang may be seen; something heavy and beige is more likely in the southwest. From long ago, the author fondly remembers catenary arches spanning the interstate and housing a glassy mid-century modern restaurant, fully in the spirit of the brave new world of speed and progress (Fig. 6.11). Somehow such confident gestures now seem to be fewer and farther between, but at least they're still out there just a bit, serving to vary the otherwise utter boredom of the interstate experience.

Many, or at least some, of the above buildings in the countryside have come to summon our admiration, or at least not to summon our dismay, so often the case with other everyday architecture. Would that these efforts were more typically the case back in the urbs and the burbs.

6.11
Glass House Restaurant, over the Will Rogers Turnpike near Vinita, Oklahoma. While the image is from long ago, the structure remains today, though renovated in the decades since and now housing – what else – a familiar fast food emporium.

most cases there has been at least a bit of an indication that all is not lost. For it's true that assorted buildings such as these don't necessarily require extra special efforts to be deserving of our attention – even our admiration. But they do require efforts as opposed to none at all: efforts by the municipality, the developer, and the community at large to expect more than the bare minimum in architectural terms, and by the designer to provide it. And while it's also true that the budget can affect the merits of everyday construction, that's hardly inevitable: design discernment and ingenuity can elevate the most modest of building projects.

While getting the job and profiting from it remain the foremost missions of those in the architectural and planning professions – and one cannot gainsay these claims, for otherwise those professionals would not be in business[1] – it's also true that their efforts are generally well meant. But such good intentions can be and often are compromised by the corporate world and its grip on development, as in fast food and big retail for starters. More independent efforts such as churches, houses, or small retail have more leeway, but thereby have more opportunities to get it wrong. It's fair to say that for all the parties involved in EA, education is both the reason for this problem (that is, in its inadequacies) and a promise for the future (for education's influence to improve).[2] Sadly enough, it's also true that not everybody chooses or even wants to be educated, so there's that.

The continued dominance of modernism, in whatever current fashion, presents another basic problem for EA, for modernism seems to work best in object buildings off by themselves, and not so well in the commercial and institutional spheres of which so much of everyday architecture consists. And while it's undeniably true

---

1   One exception that does bear mentioning would be to teach while also maintaining an office. Generally, though, one will tend to dominate and the other to end up being a sort of boutique pursuit. Another exception to the primacy of being profitable would be inherited wealth.

2   Such improvements will rely not only on advances in communication but advances in knowledge itself. Regarding architecture, whether high-style or everyday, one hopes such knowledge will increasingly concern the findings of systematic research and evidence-based design. At least it should; the author confesses to advocating the same way back in 1969 when he co-edited an issue of his alma mater's *Student Publication of the School of Design*, its articles involving such pursuits. Advances have been made since then, but not nearly enough, or widely enough understood. And ultimately such occasionally quantifiable knowledge needs to be held in equal esteem with intuitive, creative efforts, a combo that has always been and perhaps always will be hard to achieve.

that modernism has characterized many meritorious buildings, the problem is that these make up a rather small portion of what's out there.

If today's modernism is not the answer to EA's ills, we do see good efforts in a rediscovery of regional vernaculars, which appeal to us because of their recall of established norms, as opposed to modernism's lack thereof. The related recall of "main street," a durable and pleasing centerpiece for EA, affords an anchor for many of our subjects—shopping, dining, entertainment, and residential reside there comfortably, as indeed they once did in the past. And a related growth of "form based" building codes seeks to help reduce the car-centric chaos that so much commercial and residential suburbia consists of to this day. Modernism has been tried in this format and found wanting, being seemingly inharmonious with the effects of such codes, and shots across the bow of these trends from modernist camps, to the effect that they deal in nostalgia rather than authenticity, end up sounding a bit thin and, perhaps, a bit threatened. Ultimately, through such developments, much of what has been discussed here can potentially find its place in urban/suburban environments that have both order and variety; both recall and innovation. Goodness knows, there's plenty of potential in today's vast everyday wasteland.

Author Statement

The author, a retired architect, has done design work for branch banks, shopping centers, shopping malls, fast food outlets, single family houses, apartment buildings, retirement homes, car dealerships, churches, hotels, post offices, hospitals, clinics, restaurants, bars, parking facilities, office buildings, school and university buildings, dormitories, movie theaters, casinos, and entertainment centers.[1] Despite having no experience in big box stores, drugstores, gas stations, or mobile homes (though he did once design the headquarters of a major mobile home company), he feels almost qualified to have taken all these building types a bit to task. He has authored several other books: *Forming and Centering: Foundational Aspects of Architectural Design; Urban Lessons of the Venetian Squares;* and *Architecture's New Strangeness: A 21st Century Cult of Peculiarity.* This last may be considered a prequel to the present book, dealing as it does with high profile oddities of the present century, while *Everyday Architecture* deals with everything else. Following travels abroad as a Paris Prize recipient, he worked as an architect in North Carolina, Massachusetts, and Tennessee, where he helped found the architecture and planning firm BullockSmith, serving as its design director. With work nationwide and abroad, the firm has received numerous design awards despite having done a fair amount of everyday architecture.

---

1 Full disclosure, illustrations herein of architecture and planning work for which the author had principal design responsibility include numbers 2.14, 2.15, 2.19, 3.3 (upper), 3.10, 3.15, 3.23L&R, 5.8, 5.19 (lower), 6.5, 6.6, and 6.8.